D0897618

A GIFT FOR

_____

FROM

_____

Streams in the Desert®: Hope for Hurting Hearts
Copyright © 2005 by The Zondervan Corporation
ISBN-10: 0-310-98868-3
ISBN-13: 978-0-310-98868-7

All Scripture quotations, unless otherwise noted, are taken from the Holy Bible: New
International Version (North American Edition). Copyright 1973, 1978, 1984 by International
Bible Society. Used by permission of The Zondervan Corporation. All rights reserved.

The "NIV" and "New International Version" trademarks are registered in the United States
Patent and Trademark Office by International Bible Society.

This updated edition is based on the original text of *Streams in the Desert* Copyright © 1925,
1953, and 1965 by Cowman Publications, Inc., and Copyright © 1996 by Zondervan.

All rights reserved. No part of this publication may be reproduced, stored in a retrieval system,
or transmitted in any form or by any means—electronic, mechanical, photocopy, recording, or
any other—except for brief quotations in printed reviews, without the prior permission of the
publisher.

Requests for information should be addressed to:
Inspirio, the gift group of Zondervan
Grand Rapids, Michigan 49530
http://www.inspiriogifts.com

Associate Publisher: Tom Dean
Design Manager: Val Buick
Production Management: Matt Nolan
Design: The DesignWorks Group; cover, Charles Brock; interior, Charles Brock and Robin Black
        www.thedesignworksgroup.com
Cover image: Freeman Patterson/Masterfile

Printed in China
05 06 07/ SCH/ 5 4 3 2 1

streams
in the
desert®

Hope for Hurting Hearts

L. B. COWMAN
EDITED BY JIM REIMANN

inspirio™

table of contents

Essential Training for God's Divine Ministry of Comfort..10

Storms—God's Equipping School for Service 12

The Ministry of Sorrow 15

My "Ever-Present Help in Trouble" 18

Shining Through Sorrow's Dark Night...............................19

Patient Endurance for Trials 21

The Riches of Sorrow and Suffering...................................24

"The Fellowship of ... His Sufferings" 27

Triumphing in My Trials 28

The Flowers of Sorrow and Grief 31

Sorrow and the Deepest Things of Life 33

The Schools of Sorrow and Faith 35

God's Songs of Hope...38

Suffering and the Sweet Flowers of Faith...........................39

Suffering—the Father's Perfect Tool 43

Difficulties and God's Richest Blessings 45

Comfort—One of God's Most Precious Gifts 48

Divine Love and the Angel of Pain.....................................50

Brokenness and Blessings 52

The Oneness of Sorrow and Joy..54

The Trials and Triumphs of the Walk of Faith....................56

Sorrow and the Enlarging of Character 59

The Divine Mystery in Suffering............................61

Suffering, Pruning, and Abundant Fruit............................63

Adversity and a Higher View of God 65

The Prayer of Faith 67

Your Almighty Friend............................70

Passing Through the Floodwaters............................72

Without Reservation 74

Persist in Your Calling............................75

This is My Doing............................78

In the Shadow of God's Hand............................81

God Will Deliver You 83

Trials—God's School of Faith............................85

Great and Precious Promises 86

The Fact of God's Faithfulness 89

A Steadfast Anchor............................92

Keep Looking Up! 94

From Promise to Prophesy 97

Run to the Living God............................98

The Appointed Time 99

Hands Off!............................101

Stepping Out in Faith 103

Genuine Faith Indeed 106

My Grace Is Sufficient............................108

Lessons Learned Through Tears 110

He Is with Us in Trouble..112

The Blessings of Solitude 113

Mind the Checks..115

The Only Thing "Too Hard for the Lord" 117

The Arrows of God 118

A Thousand Promises..120

When We Are Tested 122

God's Time for Mercy Will Come..................................123

Wait in Quiet Patience...125

The Upper and Lower Springs 127

Suffering and the Perfecting of Character.....................130

The Secret Place 132

Delayed Answers Are Not Refusals................................134

Striking the Strings of Your Heart 136

A Constant Calm..138

Say No to "Suppose"...140

Taking Possession of God's Promises 142

Quietness in the Midst of the Raging Storm 144

The Shepherd Who "Goes On Ahead" 146

Our God—"The Living God" 148

A Steadfast Commitment to Christ................................150

The Shepherd Who is Always There 152

The Lord—Our Eternal Help 154

from the publisher

Streams in the Desert®, first published in 1925, has become one of the most beloved devotional books of all time. It has been a source of hope, encouragement, comfort, and strength for millions of people through the years.

L. B. Cowman was an American missionary in the Orient with her husband, Charles. *Streams in the Desert* is a compilation of Cowman's favorite writings from some of the best-known Christians over the last several centuries, including Charles Spurgeon, F. B. Meyer, Andrew Murray, and Hannah Whitall Smith, just to name a few. By adding appropriate Scripture passages, poems, and some of her own writings to these great truths by other great Christians, she ultimately compiled one devotional reading for each day of the year.

In this beautiful gift edition, we asked James Reimann, who edited and updated this classic, to select specific entries that would give hope to anyone experiencing a hurting heart. Rest assured that each entry was hand-selected with that goal in mind.

Our prayer is that you will find encouragement and strength within these pages. May the words and the surrounding imagery be like "streams in the desert" to you during the difficult times in your life.

THE PUBLISHER

Then will the lame leap like a deer,
and the mute tongue shout for joy.
Water will gush forth in the wilderness
and streams in the desert.

ISAIAH 35:6

essential training for
god's divine ministry of comfort

Comfort, comfort my people, says your God.
(ISAIAH 40:1)

Store up comfort. This was the prophet Isaiah's mission. The world is full of hurting and comfortless hearts. But before you will be competent for this lofty ministry, you must be trained. And your training is extremely costly, for to make it complete, you too must endure the same afflictions that are wringing countless hearts of tears and blood. Consequently, your own life becomes the hospital ward where you are taught the divine art of comfort. You will be wounded so that in the binding up of your wounds by the Great Physician, you may learn how to render first aid to the wounded everywhere.

Do you wonder why you are having to experience some great sorrow? Over the next ten years you will find many others afflicted in the same way. You will tell them how you suffered and were comforted. As the story unfolds, God will apply the anesthetic He once used on you to them. Then in the eager look followed by the gleam of hope that chases the shadow of despair from the soul, *you will know why* you were afflicted. And you will bless God for the discipline that filled your life with such a treasure of experience and helpfulness.

God comforts us not to make us comfortable but to make us *comforters.* John Henry Jowett

They tell me I must bruise
     The rose's leaf,
Ere I can keep and use
     Its fragrance brief.
They tell me I must break
     The skylark's heart,
Ere her cage song will make
     The silence start.
They tell me love must bleed,
     And friendship weep,
Ere in my deepest need
     I touch that deep.
Must it be always so
     With precious things?
Must they be bruised and go
     With beaten wings?
Ah, yes! by crushing days,
     By caging nights, by scar
Of thorn and stony ways,
     These blessings are!

storms—god's equipping school for service

A furious squall came up.

(MARK 4:37)

Some of life's storms—a great sorrow, a bitter disappointment, a crushing defeat—*suddenly* come upon us. Others may come *slowly,* appearing on the uneven edge of the horizon no larger than a person's hand. But trouble that seems so insignificant spreads until it covers the sky and overwhelms us.

Yet it is in the storm that God equips us for service. When God wants an oak tree, He plants it where the storms will shake it and the rains will beat down upon it. It is in the midnight battle with the elements that the oak develops its rugged fiber and becomes the king of the forest.

When God wants to make a person, He puts him into some storm. The history of humankind has always been rough and rugged. No one is complete until he has been out into the surge of the storm and has found the glorious fulfillment of the prayer "O God, take me, break me, make me."

A Frenchman painted a picture of universal genius. In his painting stand famous orators, philosophers, and martyrs, all of whom have achieved preeminence in various aspects of life. The remarkable fact about the picture is this: every person who is preeminent for his ability was first preeminent for suffering. In the foreground stands the figure of the man who was denied the Promised Land: Moses. Beside him, feeling his way, is blind Homer. Milton is there, blind and heartbroken. Then there is the form of One who towers above them all. What is His characteristic? His face is marred more than any other. The artist might have titled that great picture *The Storm.*

The beauties of nature come after the storm. The rugged beauty of the mountain is born in a storm, and the heroes of life are the storm-swept and battle-scarred.

You have been in the storms and swept by the raging winds. Have they left you broken, weary, and beaten in the valley, or have they lifted you to the sunlit summits of a richer, deeper, more abiding manhood or womanhood? Have they left you with more sympathy for the storm-swept and the battle-scarred?

The wind that blows can never kill
     The tree God plants;
It blows toward east, and then toward west,
The tender leaves have little rest,
But any wind that blows is best.
     The tree that God plants
Strikes deeper root, grows higher still,
Spreads greater limbs, for God's good will
     Meets all its wants.
There is no storm has power to blast
     The tree God knows;
No thunderbolt, nor beating rain,
Nor lightning flash, nor hurricane;
When they are spent, it does remain,
     The tree God knows.
Through every storm it still stands fast,
And from its first day to its last
     Still fairer grows.

the ministry of sorrow

Sorrow is better than laughter, because a sad face is good for the heart.
(ECCLESIASTES 7:3)

Sorrow, under the power of divine grace, performs various ministries in our lives. Sorrow reveals unknown depths of the soul, and unknown capacities for suffering and service. Lighthearted, frivolous people are always shallow and are never aware of their own meagerness or lack of depth. Sorrow is God's tool to plow the depths of the soul, that it may yield richer harvests.

If humankind were still in a glorified state, having never fallen, then the strong floods of divine joy would be the force God would use to reveal our souls' capacities. But in a fallen world, sorrow, yet with despair removed, is the power chosen to reveal us to ourselves. Accordingly, it is sorrow that causes us to take the time to think deeply and seriously.

Sorrow makes us move more slowly and considerately and examine our motives and attitudes. It opens within us the capacities of the heavenly life, and it makes us willing to set our capacities afloat on a limitless sea of service for God and for others.

Imagine a village of lazy people living at the foot of a great mountain range, yet who have never ventured out to explore

the valleys and canyons back in the mountains. One day a great thunderstorm goes careening through the mountains, turning the hidden valleys into echoing trumpets and revealing their inner recesses, like the twisted shapes of a giant seashell. The villagers at the foot of the hills are astonished at the labyrinths and the unexplored recesses of a region so nearby and yet so unknown. And so it is with many people who casually live on the outer edge of their own souls until great thunderstorms of sorrow reveal hidden depths within, which were never before known or suspected.

God never uses anyone to a great degree until He breaks the person completely. Joseph experienced more sorrow than the other sons of Jacob, and it led him into a ministry of food for all the nations. For this reason, the Holy Spirit said of him, "Joseph is a fruitful vine ... near a spring, whose branches climb over a wall" (Gen. 49:22). It takes sorrow to expand and deepen the soul. FROM THE HEAVENLY LIFE

The dark brown soil is turned
By the sharp-pointed plow;
And I've a lesson learned.
My life is but a field,
Stretched out beneath God's sky,
Some harvest rich to yield.
Where grows the golden grain?
Where faith? Where sympathy?
In a furrow cut by pain.

MALTBIE D. BABCOCK

Every person and every nation must endure lessons in God's school of adversity. In the same way we say, "Blessed is the night, for it reveals the stars to us," we can say, "Blessed is sorrow, for it reveals God's comfort." A flood once washed away a poor man's home and mill, taking with it everything he owned in the world. He stood at the scene of his great loss, brokenhearted and discouraged. Yet after the waters had subsided, he saw something shining in the riverbanks that the flood had washed bare. "It looks like gold," he said. And it was gold. The storm that had impoverished him made him rich. So it is oftentimes in life. HENRY CLAY TRUMBULL

MY "EVER-PRESENT HELP IN TROUBLE"

Why, O Lord, do you stand far off?
(PSALM 10:1)

"God is ... an ever-present help in trouble" (Ps. 46:1). But He allows trouble to pursue us, as though He were indifferent to its overwhelming pressure, so we may be brought to the end of ourselves. Through the trial, we are led to discover the treasure of darkness and the immeasurable wealth of tribulation.

We may be sure that He who allows the suffering is with us throughout it. It may be that we will only see Him once the ordeal is nearly passed, but we must dare to believe that He never leaves our trial. Our eyes are blinded so we cannot see the One our soul loves. The darkness and our bandages blind us so that we cannot see the form of our High Priest. Yet He is there and is deeply touched.

Let us not rely on our feelings but trust in His unswerving faithfulness. And though we cannot see Him, let us talk to Him. Although His presence is veiled, once we begin to speak to Jesus as if He were literally present, an answering voice comes to show us He is in the shadow, keeping watch over His own. Your Father is as close to you when you journey through the darkest tunnel as He is when you are under the open heaven!

FROM DAILY DEVOTIONAL COMMENTARY

Although the path be all unknown?
Although the way be drear?
Its shades I travel not alone
When steps of Yours are near.

shining through sorrow's dark night

He turned the sea into dry land, they passed through the waters on foot—come, let us rejoice in him.

(PSALM 66:6)

It is a profound statement that "through *the waters,*" the very place where we might have expected nothing but trembling, terror, anguish, and dismay, the children of Israel stopped to "rejoice in him"!

How many of us can relate to this experience? Who of us, right in the midst of our time of distress and sadness, have been able to triumph and rejoice, as the Israelites did?

How close God is to us through His promises, and how brightly those promises shine! Yet during times of prosperity, we lose sight of their brilliance. In the way the sun at noon hides the stars from sight, His promises become indiscernible. But when night falls—the deep, dark night of sorrow—a host of stars begin to shine, bringing forth God's blessed constellations of hope, and promises of comfort from His Word.

Just as Jacob experienced at Jabbok, it is only once the sun sets that the Angel of the Lord comes, wrestles with us, and we can overcome. It was at night, "at twilight" (Ex. 30:8), that Aaron lit the sanctuary lamps. And it is often during nights of trouble that the brightest lamps of believers are set ablaze.

It was during a dark time of loneliness and exile that John had the glorious vision of his Redeemer. Many of us today have our "Isle of Patmos," which produces the brightest memories of God's enduring presence, uplifting grace, and love in spite of solitude and sadness.

How many travelers today, still passing through their Red Seas and Jordan Rivers of earthly affliction, will be able to look back from eternity, filled with memories of God's great goodness, and say, "We 'passed through the waters on foot.' And yet, even in these dark experiences, with waves surging all around, we stopped and said, 'Let us rejoice in him'!" J. R. Macduff

There I will give her back her vineyards, and will make the Valley of Achor a door of hope. *There* she will sing. Hosea 2:15

patient endurance for trials

Although I have afflicted you,...
I will afflict you no more.
(NAHUM 1:12)

There is a limit to our affliction. God sends it and then removes it. Do you complain, saying, "When will this end?" May we quietly wait and patiently endure the will of the Lord till He comes. Our Father takes away the rod when His purpose in using it is fully accomplished.

If the affliction is sent to test us so that our words would glorify God, it will only end once He has caused us to testify to His praise and honor. In fact, we would not want the difficulty to depart until God has removed from us all the honor we can yield to Him.

Today things may become "completely calm" (Matt. 8:26). Who knows how soon these raging waves will give way to a sea of glass with seagulls sitting on the gentle swells?

After a long ordeal, the threshing tool is on its hook, and the wheat has been gathered into the barn. Before much time has passed, we may be just as happy as we are sorrowful now.

It is not difficult for the Lord to turn night into day. He who sends the clouds can just as easily clear the skies. Let us be encouraged—things are better down the road. *Let us sing God's praises in anticipation of things to come.* CHARLES H. SPURGEON

"The Lord of the harvest" (Luke 10:2) is not always threshing us. His trials are only for a season, and the showers soon pass. "Weeping may remain for a night, but rejoicing comes in the morning" (Ps. 30:5). "Our light and momentary troubles are achieving for us an eternal glory that far outweighs them all" (2 Cor. 4:17). Trials do serve their purpose.

Even the fact that we face a trial proves there is something very precious to our Lord in us, or else He would not spend so much time and energy on us. Christ would not test us if He did not see the precious metal of faith mingled with the rocky core of our nature, and it is to refine us into purity and beauty that He forces us through the fiery ordeal.

Be patient, O sufferer! The result of the Refiner's fire will more than compensate for our trials, once we see the "eternal glory that far outweighs them all." Just to hear His commendation, "Well done" (Matt. 25:21); to be honored before the holy angels; to be glorified in Christ, so that I may reflect His glory back to Him—ah! that will be more than enough reward for all my trials. FROM TRIED BY FIRE

Just as the weights of a grandfather clock, or the stabilizers in a ship, are necessary for them to work properly, so are troubles to the soul. The sweetest perfumes are obtained only through tremendous pressure, the fairest flowers grow on the most isolated and snowy peaks, the most beautiful gems are those that have suffered the longest at the jeweler's wheel, and the most magnificent statues have endured the most blows from the chisel. All of these, however, are subject to God's law. Nothing happens that has not been *appointed* with consummate care and foresight. FROM DAILY DEVOTIONAL COMMENTARY

The Riches of sorrow and suffering

After the death of Moses the servant of the Lord,
the Lord said to Joshua son of Nun, Moses' aide:
"Moses my servant is dead. Now then, you and all
these people, get ready to cross the Jordan River."
(JOSHUA 1:1–2)

Yesterday you experienced a great sorrow, and now your home seems empty. Your first impulse is to give up and to sit down in despair amid your dashed hopes. Yet you must defy that temptation, for you are at the front line of the battle, and the crisis is at hand. Faltering even one moment would put God's interest at risk. Other lives will be harmed by your hesitation, and His work will suffer if you simply fold your hands. You must not linger at this point, even to indulge your grief.

A famous general once related this sorrowful story from his own wartime experience. His son was the lieutenant of an artillery unit, and an assault was in progress. As the father led his division in a charge, pressing on across the battlefield, suddenly his eye caught sight of a dead artillery officer lying right before him. Just a glance told him it was his son. The general's fatherly impulse was to kneel by the body of his beloved son and express his grief, but the duty of the moment demanded he press on with his charge. So after quickly kissing his dead son, he hurried away, leading his command in the assault.

Weeping inconsolably beside a grave will never bring back the treasure of a lost love, nor can any blessing come from such great sadness. Sorrow causes deep scars, and indelibly writes its story on the suffering heart. We never completely recover from our greatest griefs and are never exactly the same after having passed through them. Yet sorrow that is endured in the right spirit impacts our growth favorably and brings us a greater sense of compassion for others. Indeed, those who have no scars of sorrow or suffering upon them are poor.

"The joy set before" (Heb. 12:2) us should shine on our griefs just as the sun shines through the clouds, making them radiant. God has ordained our truest and richest comfort to be found by pressing on toward the goal. Sitting down and brooding over our sorrow deepens the darkness surrounding us, allowing it to creep into our hearts. And soon our strength has changed to weakness. But if we will turn from the gloom and remain faithful to the calling of God, the light will shine again and we will grow stronger. J. R. MILLER

Lord, You know that through our tears
    Of hasty, selfish weeping
Comes surer sin, and for our petty fears
    Of loss You have in keeping
A greater gain than all of which we dreamed;
    You knowest that in grasping
The bright possessions which so precious seemed
    We lose them; but if, clasping
Your faithful hand, we tread with steadfast feet
    The path of Your appointing,
There waits for us a treasury of sweet
    Delight, royal anointing
With oil of gladness and of strength.

HELEN HUNT JACKSON

"The fellowship of...His sufferings"

Dear friends, do not be surprised at the painful trial you are suffering.... But rejoice that you participate in the sufferings of Christ.

(1 PETER 4:12–13)

Many hours of waiting were necessary to enrich David's harp with song. And hours of waiting in the wilderness will provide us with psalms of "thanksgiving and the sound of singing" (Isa. 51:3). The hearts of the discouraged here below will be lifted, and joy will be brought to our Father's heavenly home.

What was the preparation for Jesse's son, David, to compose songs unlike any others ever heard before on earth? It was the sinful persecution he endured at the hands of the wicked that brought forth his cries for God's help. Then David's faint hope in God's goodness blossomed into full songs of rejoicing, declaring the Lord's mighty deliverances and multiplied mercies. Every sorrow was yet another note from his harp, and every deliverance another theme of praise.

One stinging sorrow spared would have been one blessing missed and unclaimed. One difficulty or danger escaped—how great would have been our loss! The thrilling psalms where God's people today find expression for their grief or praise might never have been known.

Waiting on God and abiding in His will is to know Him in "the fellowship of sharing in his sufferings" (Phil. 3:10) and "to be conformed to the likeness of his Son" (Rom. 8:29). Therefore if God's desire is to enlarge your capacity for spiritual understanding, do not be frightened by the greater realm of suffering that awaits you. The Lord's capacity for sympathy is greater still, for the breath of the Holy Spirit into His new creation never makes a heart hard and insensitive, but affectionate, tender, and true. ANNA SHIPTON

I thank Christ Jesus our Lord,
who has given me strength, that he considered me
faithful, appointing me to his service.
(1 TIMOTHY 1:12)

Triumphing in My Trials

Glorify ye the LORD in the fires.
(ISAIAH 24:15 KJV)

Notice the little word "in"! We are to honor the Lord *in* the trial—*in* the very thing that afflicts us. And although there are examples where God did not allow His saints to even feel the fire, usually the fire causes pain.

It is precisely there, in the heat of the fire, we are to glorify Him. We do this by exercising perfect faith in His goodness and love that has permitted this trial to come upon us. Even more, we are to believe that out of the fire will arise something more worthy of praise to Him than had we never experienced it.

To go through some fires will take great faith, for little faith will fail. We must win the victory *in* the furnace.

A person has only as much faith as he shows in times of trouble. The three men who were thrown into the fiery furnace came out just as they went in—*except for the ropes* that had bound them. How often God removes our shackles in the furnace of affliction!

These three men walked through the fire unhurt—their skin was not even blistered. Not only had the fire "not harmed their bodies, nor was a hair of their heads singed; their robes were not scorched, and there was no smell of fire on them" (Dan. 3:27).

This is the way Christians should come out of the furnace of fiery trials—liberated from their shackles but untouched by the flames.

He made a show of them openly, triumphing over them in it (Colossians 2:15 KJV). This is the real triumph—triumphing over sickness *in it,* triumphing over death *in* dying, and triumphing over other adverse circumstances *in* them. Believe me, there is a power that can make us victors *in* the conflict.

There are heights we can reach where we can look back over the path we have come and sing our song of triumph on this side of heaven. We can cause others to regard us as rich, while we are poor, and make many rich in our poverty. We are to triumph *in it*.

Christ's triumph was *in* His humiliation. And perhaps our triumph will also be revealed through what others see as humiliation. MARGARET BOTTOME

Isn't there something captivating about the sight of a person burdened with many trials, yet who is as lighthearted as the sound of a bell? Isn't there something contagious and valiant in seeing others who are greatly tempted but are "more than conquerors" (Rom. 8:37)? Isn't it heartening to see a fellow traveler whose body is broken, yet who retains the splendor of unbroken patience?

What a witness these give to the power of God's gift of grace! JOHN HENRY JOWETT

When each earthly brace falls under,
*   And life seems a restless sea,*
Are you then a God-held wonder,
*   Satisfied and calm and free?*

The flowers of sorrow and Grief

Mary Magdalene and the other Mary were sitting there opposite the tomb.
(MATTHEW 27:61)

Oh, how slow grief is to come to understanding! Grief is ignorant and does not even care to learn. When the grieving women "were sitting there opposite the tomb," did they see the triumph of the next two thousand years? Did they see anything except that Christ was gone?

The Christ you and I know today came from their loss. Countless mourning hearts have since seen resurrection in the midst of their grief, and yet these sorrowing women watched at the beginning of this result and saw nothing. What they regarded as the end of life was actually the preparation for coronation, for Christ remained silent that He might live again with tenfold power.

They did not see it. They mourned, wept, went away, and then came again to the sepulcher, driven by their broken hearts. And still it was only a tomb—unprophetic, voiceless, and drab.

It is the same with us. Each of us sits "opposite the tomb" in our own garden and initially says, "This tragedy is irreparable. I see no benefit in it and will take no comfort in it." And yet right in the midst of our deepest and worst adversities, our Christ is often just lying there, waiting to be resurrected.

Our Savior is where our death seems to be. At the end of our hope, we find the brightest beginning of fulfillment. Where darkness seems the deepest, the most radiant light is set to emerge. And once the experience is complete, we find our garden is not disfigured by the tomb.

Our joys are made better when sorrow is in the midst of them. And our sorrows become bright through the joys God has planted around them. At first the flowers of the garden may not appear to be our favorites, but we will learn that they are the flowers of the heart. The flowers planted at the grave deep within the Christian heart are love, hope, faith, joy, and peace.

'Twas by a path of sorrows drear
*   Christ entered into rest;*
And shall I look for roses here,
*   Or think that earth is blessed?*
*   Heaven's whitest lilies blow*
*   From earth's sharp crown of woe:*
Who here his cross can meekly bear,
Shall wear the kingly purple there.

sorrow and the deepest things of life

*I endure everything for the sake of the elect,
that they too may obtain the salvation that is in
Christ Jesus, with eternal glory.*
(2 TIMOTHY 2:10)

Oh, if only Job had known, as he sat in the ashes, troubling his heart over the thought of God's providence, that millions down through history would look back on his trials. He might have taken courage in the fact that his experience would be a help to others throughout the world.

No one lives to himself, and Job's story is like yours and mine, only his was written for all to see. The afflictions Job faced and the trials he wrestled with are the very things for which he is remembered, and without them we would probably never have read of him in God's Word.

We never know the trials that await us in the days ahead. We may not be able to see the light through our struggles, but we can believe that those days, as in the life of Job, will be the most significant we are called upon to live. ROBERT COLLYER

Who has not learned that our most sorrowful days are frequently our best? The days when our face is full of smiles and we skip easily through the soft meadow God has adorned with spring flowers, the capacity of our heart is often wasted.

The soul that is always lighthearted and cheerful misses the deepest things of life. Certainly that life has its reward and is fully satisfied, but the depth of its satisfaction is very shallow. Its heart is dwarfed, and its nature, which has the potential of experiencing the highest heights and the deepest depths, remains undeveloped. And the wick of its life burns quickly to the bottom, without ever knowing the richness of profound joy.

Remember, Jesus said, "Blessed are those who mourn" (Matt. 5:4). Stars shine the brightest during the long dark night of winter. And the gentian wildflowers display their fairest blooms among the nearly inaccessible heights of mountain snow and ice.

God seems to use the pressure of pain to trample out the fulfillment of His promises and thereby release the sweetest juice of His winepress. Only those who have known sorrow can fully appreciate the great tenderness of the "man of sorrows" (Isa. 53:3).

You may be experiencing little sunshine, but the long periods of gloomy darkness have been wisely designed for you, for perhaps a lengthy stretch of summer weather would have made you like parched land or a barren wilderness. Your Lord knows best, and the clouds and the sun wait for His command.

When told, "It's a gray day," an old Scottish cobbler once replied, "Yes, but didn't ya see the patch of blue?"

the schools of sorrow and faith

*Against all hope, Abraham in hope believed....
without weakening in his faith.*
(ROMANS 4:18–19)

I will never forget the statement which that great man of faith George Mueller once made to a gentleman who had asked him the best way to have strong faith: "The *only* way to know strong faith is to endure great trials. I have learned my faith by standing firm through severe testings."

How true this is! *You must trust when all else fails.*

Dear soul, you may scarcely realize the value of your present situation. If you are enduring great afflictions right now, you are at the source of the strongest faith. God will teach you during these dark hours to have the most powerful bond to His throne you could ever know, if you will only submit.

"Don't be afraid; just believe" (Mark 5:36). But if you ever are afraid, simply look up and say, "When I am afraid, I will trust in you" (Ps. 56:3). Then you will be able to thank God for His school of sorrow that became for you the school of faith. A. B. SIMPSON

Great faith must first endure great trials. God's greatest gifts come through great pain. Can we find anything of value in the spiritual or the natural realm that has come about without tremendous toil and tears? Has there ever been any great reform, any discovery benefiting humankind, or any soul-awakening revival, without the diligence and the shedding of blood of those whose sufferings were actually the pangs of its birth? For the temple of God to be built, David had to bear intense afflictions. And for the gospel of grace to be extricated from Jewish tradition, Paul's life had to be one long agony.

Take heart, O weary, burdened one, bowed down
    Beneath your cross;
Remember that your greatest gain may come
    Through greatest loss.
Your life is nobler for a sacrifice,
    And more divine.
Acres of blooms are crushed to make a drop
    Of perfume fine.
Because of storms that lash the ocean waves,
    The waters there
Keep purer than if the heavens o'erhead
    Were always fair.
The brightest banner of the skies floats not
    At noonday warm;
The rainbow follows after thunderclouds,
    And after storm.

god's songs of hope

Where is God my Maker, who gives songs in the night?
(JOB 35:10)

Do you ever experience sleepless nights, tossing and turning and simply waiting for the first glimmer of dawn? When that happens, why not ask the Holy Spirit to fix your thoughts on God, your Maker, and believe He can fill those lonely, dreary nights with song?

Is your night one of bereavement? Focusing on God often causes Him to draw near to your grieving heart, bringing you the assurance that He needs the one who has died. The Lord will assure you He has called the eager, enthusiastic spirit of your departed loved one to stand with the invisible yet liberated, living, and radiant multitude. And as this thought enters your mind, along with the knowledge that your loved one is engaged in a great heavenly mission, a song begins in your heart.

Is your night one of discouragement or failure, whether real or imagined? Do you feel as if no one understands you, and your friends have pushed you aside? Take heart: your Maker "will come near to you" (James 4:8) and give you a song—a song of hope, which will be harmonious with the strong, resonant music of His providence. Be ready to sing the song your Maker imparts to you.

What then? Shall we sit idly down and say
The night has come; it is no longer day?
Yet as the evening twilight fades away,
The sky is filled with stars, invisible to day.

The strength of a ship is only fully demonstrated when it faces a hurricane, and the power of the gospel can only be fully exhibited when a Christian is subjected to some fiery trial. We must understand that for God to give "songs in the night," He must first make it night. NATHANIEL WILLIAM TAYLOR

suffering and the sweet flowers of faith

God has made me fruitful in the land of my suffering.
(GENESIS 41:52)

A poet stands by the window watching a summer shower. It is a fierce downpour, beating and pounding the earth. But the poet, in his mind's eye, sees more than a rain shower falling. He sees a myriad of lovely flowers raining down, soon breaking forth from the freshly watered earth, and filling it with their matchless beauty and fragrance. And so he sings:

It isn't raining rain to me—it's raining daffodils;
In every dripping drop I see wildflowers upon
        the hills.
A cloud of gray engulfs the day, and overwhelms
        the town;
It isn't raining rain to me—it's raining roses down.

Perhaps you are undergoing some trial as God's child, and you are saying to Him, "O God, it is raining very hard on me tonight, and this test seems beyond my power to endure. Disappointments are pouring in, washing away and utterly defeating my chosen plans. My trembling heart is grieved and is cowering at the intensity of my suffering. Surely the rains of affliction are beating down upon my soul."

Dear friend, you are completely mistaken. God is not raining rain on you—*He is raining blessings.* If you will only believe your Father's Word, you will realize that springing up beneath the pounding rain are spiritual flowers. And they are more beautiful and fragrant than those that ever grew before in your stormless and suffering-free life.

You can see the rain, but can you also see the flowers? You are suffering through these tests, but know that God sees sweet flowers of faith springing up in your life beneath these very trials. You try to escape the pain, yet God sees tender compassion for other sufferers finding birth in your soul.

Your heart winces at the pain of heavy grief, but God sees the sorrow deepening and enriching your life.

No, my friend, it is not raining afflictions on you. It is raining tenderness, love, compassion, patience, and a thousand other flowers and fruits of the blessed Holy Spirit. And they are bringing to your life spiritual enrichment that all the prosperity and ease of this world could never produce in your innermost being. J. M. M.

Songs across the Storm

A harp stood in the calm, still air,
Where showers of sunshine washed a thousand
    fragrant blooms;
A traveler bowed with loads of care
Struggled from morning till the dusk of evening glooms
To strum sweet sounds from the songless strings;
The pilgrim strives in vain with each unanswering chord,
Until the tempest's thunder sings,
And, moving on the storm, the fingers of the Lord
A wondrous melody awakes;
And though the battling winds their soldier deeds perform,
Their trumpet-sound brave music makes
While God's assuring voice sings love across the storm.

suffering—The father's perfect Tool

Shall I not drink the cup the Father has given me?
(JOHN 18:11)

To "drink the cup" was a greater thing than calming the seas or raising the dead. The prophets and apostles could do amazing miracles, but they did not always do the will of God and thereby suffered as a result. Doing God's will and thus experiencing suffering is still the highest form of faith, and the most glorious Christian achievement.

Having your brightest aspirations as a young person forever crushed; bearing burdens daily that are always difficult, and never seeing relief; finding yourself worn down by poverty while simply desiring to do good for others and provide a comfortable living for those you love; being shackled by an incurable physical disability; being completely alone, separated from all those you love, to face the trauma of life alone; yet in all these, still being able to say through such a difficult school of discipline, "Shall I not drink the cup the Father has given me?"— this is faith at its highest, and spiritual success at its crowning point.

Great faith is exhibited not so much in doing as in suffering.

CHARLES PARKHURST

In order to have a sympathetic God, we must have a suffering Savior, for true sympathy comes from understanding another person's hurt by suffering the same affliction. Therefore we cannot help others who suffer without paying a price ourselves, because afflictions are the cost we pay for our ability to sympathize. Those who wish to help others must first suffer. If we wish to rescue others, we must be willing to face the cross; experiencing the greatest happiness in life through ministering to others is impossible without drinking the cup Jesus drank and without submitting to the baptism He endured.

The most comforting of David's psalms were squeezed from his life by suffering, and if Paul had not been given "a thorn in the flesh" (2 Cor. 12:7 KJV), we would have missed much of the heartbeat of tenderness that resonates through so many of his letters.

If you have surrendered yourself to Christ, your present circumstances that seem to be pressing so hard against you are the perfect tool in the Father's hand to chisel you into shape for eternity. So trust Him and never push away the instrument He is using, or you will miss the result of His work in your life.

Strange and difficult indeed
    We may find it,
But the blessing that we need
    Is behind it.
The school of suffering graduates exceptional scholars.

Difficulties and God's Richest Blessings

*Have you entered the storehouses ... which I reserve
for times of trouble?*
(JOB 38:22–23)

Our trials are great opportunities, but all too often we simply
see them as large obstacles. If only we would recognize every
difficult situation as something God has chosen to prove His
love to us, each obstacle would then become a place of shelter
and rest, and a demonstration to others of His inexpressible
power. If we would look for the signs of His glorious handiwork,
then every cloud would indeed become a rainbow, and every
difficult mountain path would become one of ascension,
transformation, and glorification.

If we would look at our past, most of us would realize that
the times we endured the greatest stress and felt that every path
was blocked were the very times our heavenly Father chose to
do the kindest things for us and bestow His richest blessings.

God's most beautiful jewels are often delivered in rough packages by very difficult people, but within the package we will find the very treasures of the King's palace and the Bridegroom's love. A. B. SIMPSON

We must trust the Lord through the darkness, and honor Him with unwavering confidence even in the midst of difficult situations. The reward of this kind of faith will be like that of an eagle shedding its feathers is said to receive—a renewed sense of youth and strength. J. R. MACDUFF

If we could see beyond today
*   As God can see;*
If all the clouds should roll away,
*   The shadows flee;*
O'er present griefs we would not fret.
Each sorrow we would soon forget,
For many joys are waiting yet
*   For you and me.*
If we could know beyond today
*   As God does know,*
Why dearest treasures pass away
*   And tears must flow;*
And why the darkness leads to light,
Why dreary paths will soon grow bright;

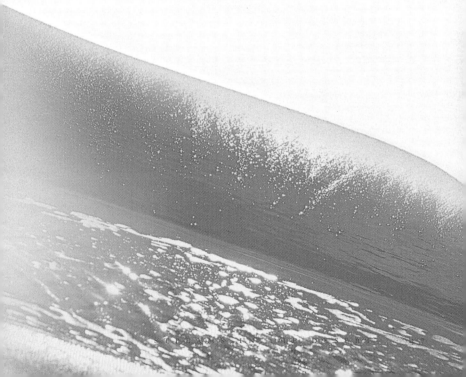

Some day life's wrongs will be made right,
Faith tells us so.
"If we could see, if we could know,"
We often say,
But God in love a veil does throw
Across our way;
We cannot see what lies before,
And so we cling to Him the more,
He leads us till this life is o'er;
Trust and obey.

comfort—one of God's most precious gifts

Blessed are those whose strength is in you....
As they pass through the Valley of Baca, they make
it a place of springs.
(PSALM 84:5–6)

Comfort is not given to us when we are lighthearted and cheerful. We must travel the depths of emotion in order to experience comfort—one of God's most precious gifts. And then we must be prepared to become coworkers with Him.

When the shadows of night—needed night—gather over the garden of our souls, when leaves close up and flowers no longer reflect any sunlight within their folded petals, and when we experience even the thickest darkness, we must remember that we will never be found wanting and that the comforting drops of heavenly dew fall only after the sun has set.

I have been through the valley of weeping,
*   The valley of sorrow and pain;*
But the "God of all comfort" was with me,
*   At hand to uphold and sustain.*
As the earth needs the clouds and sunshine,
*   Our souls need both sorrow and joy;*

So He places us oft in the furnace,
  The dross from the gold to destroy.
When he leads through some valley of trouble,
  His omnipotent hand we trace;
For the trials and sorrows He sends us
  Are part of His lessons in grace.
Oft we run from the purging and pruning,
  Forgetting the Gardener knows
That the deeper the cutting and trimming,
  The richer the cluster that grows.
Well He knows that affliction is needed;
  He has a wise purpose in view,
And in the dark valley He whispers,
  "Soon you'll understand what I do."
As we travel through life's shadowed valley,
  Fresh springs of His love ever rise;
And we learn that our sorrows and losses
  Are blessings just sent in disguise.
So we'll follow wherever He leads us,
  Let the path be dreary or bright;
For we've proved that our God can give comfort;
  Our God can give songs in the night.

Divine Love and the Angel of Pain

Yet when he heard that Lazarus was sick,
he stayed where he was two more days.
(JOHN 11:6)

This miraculous story begins with the following declaration: "Jesus loved Martha and her sister and Lazarus" (v. 5). It is as if God were teaching us that at the very heart and foundation of all His dealings with us, no matter how dark and mysterious they may be, we must dare to believe in and affirm His infinite, unmerited, and unchanging love. Yet love permits pain to occur.

Mary and Martha never doubted that Jesus would quickly avert every obstacle to keep their brother from death, "yet when he heard that Lazarus was sick, he stayed where he was two more days."

What a startling word: *"Yet"*! Jesus refrained from going not because He did not love them but because He *did* love them. It was His love alone that kept Him from hurrying at once to their beloved yet grief-stricken home. Anything less than infinite love would have rushed instantly to the relief of those beloved and troubled hearts, in an effort to end their grief, to have the blessing of wiping and stopping the flow of their tears, and to cause their sorrow and pain to flee. Only the power of divine love could have held back the spontaneity of the Savior's tenderheartedness until the angel of pain had finished his work.

Who can estimate the great debt we owe to suffering and pain? If not for them, we would have little capacity for many of the great virtues of the Christian life. Where would our faith be if not for the trials that test it; or patience, without anything to endure or experience and without tribulations to develop it?

Loved! then the way will not be drear;
For One we know is ever near,
Proving it to our hearts so clear
    That we are loved.
Loved when our sky is clouded o'er,
And days of sorrow press us sore;
Still we will trust Him evermore,
    For we are loved.
Time, that affects all things below,
Can never change the love He'll show;
The heart of Christ with love will flow,
    And we are loved.

Brokenness and Blessings

We must go through many hardships to enter
the kingdom of God.
(ACTS 14:22)

The best things in life are the result of being wounded. Wheat must be crushed before becoming bread, and incense must be burned by fire before its fragrance is set free. The earth must be broken with a sharp plow before being ready to receive the seed. And it is a broken heart that pleases God.

Yes, the sweetest joys of life are the fruits of sorrow. Human nature seems to need suffering to make it fit to be a blessing to the world.

Beside my cottage door it grows,
The loveliest, daintiest flower that blows,
  A sweetbrier rose.
At dewy morn or twilight's close,
The rarest perfume from it flows,
  This strange wild rose.
But when the raindrops on it beat,
Ah, then, its odors grow more sweet,
  About my feet.
Often with loving tenderness,

Its soft green leaves I gently press,
In sweet caress.
A still more wondrous fragrance flows
The more my fingers close
And crush the rose.
Dear Lord, oh, let my life be so
Its perfume when strong winds blow,
The sweeter flow.
And should it be Your blessed will,
With crushing grief my soul to fill,
Press harder still.
And while its dying fragrance flows
I'll whisper low, "He loves and knows
His crushed brier rose."

If you aspire to be a person of consolation, if you want to share the priestly gift of sympathy, if you desire to go beyond giving commonplace comfort to a heart that is tempted, and if you long to go through the daily exchanges of life with the kind of tact that never inflicts pain, then you must be prepared to pay the price for a costly education—for like Christ, you must suffer. FREDERICK WILLIAM ROBERTSON

The oneness of sorrow and joy

. . . sorrowful, yet always rejoicing.
(2 CORINTHIANS 6:10)

Sorrow was beautiful, but his beauty was the beauty of the moonlight shining through the leafy branches of the trees in the woods. His gentle light made little pools of silver here and there on the soft green moss of the forest floor. And when he sang, his song was like the low, sweet calls of the nightingale, and in his eyes was the unexpectant gaze of someone who has ceased to look for coming gladness. He could weep in tender sympathy with those who weep, but to rejoice with those who rejoice was unknown to him.

Joy was beautiful, too, but hers was the radiant beauty of a summer morning. Her eyes still held the happy laughter of childhood, and her hair glistened with the sunshine's kiss. When she sang, her voice soared upward like a skylark's, and her steps were the march of a conqueror who has never known defeat. She could rejoice with anyone who rejoices, but to weep with those who weep was unknown to her.

Sorrow longingly said, "We can never be united as one." "No, never," responded Joy, with eyes misting as she spoke, "for *my* path lies through the sunlit meadows, the sweetest roses bloom when I arrive, and songbirds await my coming to sing their most joyous melodies."

"Yes, and *my* path," said Sorrow, turning slowly away, "leads through the dark forest, and moonflowers, which open only at night, will fill my hands. Yet the sweetest of all earthly songs—the love song of the night—will be mine. So farewell, dear Joy, farewell."

Yet even as Sorrow spoke, he and Joy became aware of someone standing beside them. In spite of the dim light, they sensed a kingly Presence, and suddenly a great and holy awe overwhelmed them. They then sank to their knees before Him.

"I see Him as the King of Joy," whispered Sorrow, "for on His head are many crowns, and the nailprints in His hands and feet are the scars of a great victory. And before Him all my sorrow is melting away into deathless love and gladness. I now give myself to Him forever."

"No, Sorrow," said Joy softly, "for I see Him as the King of Sorrow, and the crown on His head is a crown of thorns, and the nailprints in His hands and feet are the scars of terrible agony. I also give myself to Him forever, for sorrow with Him must be sweeter than any joy I have ever known."

"Then we are *one* in Him," they cried in gladness, "for no one but He could unite Joy and Sorrow." Therefore they walked hand in hand into the world, to follow Him through storms and sunshine, through winter's severe cold and the warmth of summer's gladness, and to be "sorrowful, yet always rejoicing."

Does Sorrow lay his hand upon your shoulder,
   And walk with you in silence on life's way,
While Joy, your bright companion once, grown colder,
   Becomes to you more distant day by day?
Run not from the companionship of Sorrow,
   He is the messenger of God to thee;
And you will thank Him in His great tomorrow—
   For what you do not know now, you then will see;
He is God's angel, clothed in veils of night,
With whom "we walk by faith" and "not by sight."

The Trials and Triumphs of the Walk of Faith

The rest were to get there on planks or on pieces of the ship. In this way everyone reached land in safety.
(ACTS 27:44)

The miraculous story of Paul's voyage to Rome, with its trials and triumphs, is a wonderful example of the light and the darkness through the journey of faith of human life. And the most remarkable part of the journey is the difficult and narrow places that are interspersed with God's extraordinary providence and intervention.

It is a common misconception that the Christian's walk of faith is strewn with flowers and that when God intervenes in the lives of His people, He does so in such a wonderful way as to always lift us out of our difficult surroundings. In actual fact, however, the real experience is quite the opposite. And the message of the Bible is one of alternating trials and triumphs in the lives of "a great cloud of witnesses" (Heb. 12:1), everyone from Abel to the last martyr.

Paul, more than anyone else, is an example of how much a child of God can suffer without being defeated or broken in spirit. Because of his testimony given in Damascus, he was hunted down by persecutors and forced to flee for his life. Yet we see no heavenly chariot, amid lightning bolts of fire, coming to rescue the holy apostle from the hands of his enemies. God instead worked a simple way of escape for Paul: "His followers took him by night and lowered him in a basket through an opening in the wall" (Acts 9:25). Yes, he was in an old clothes basket, like a bundle of laundry or groceries. The servant of the Lord Jesus Christ was lowered from a window over the wall of Damascus, and in a humble way escaped the hatred of his foes.

Later we find him languishing for months in lonely dungeons, telling of his "sleepless nights and hunger" (2 Cor. 6:5), of being deserted by friends, and of his brutal, humiliating beatings. And even after God promised to deliver him, we see him left for days to toss upon a stormy sea and compelled to protect a treacherous sailor. And finally, once his deliverance comes, it is not by way of some heavenly ship sailing from the skies to rescue this illustrious prisoner. Nor is there an angel who comes walking on the water to still the raging sea. There is no supernatural sign at all of surpassing greatness being carried out, for one man is required to grab a piece of the mast to survive, another a floating timber, another a small fragment of the shipwreck, and yet another is forced to swim for his life.

In this account, we also find God's pattern for our own lives. It is meant to be good news to those who live in this everyday world in ordinary surroundings and who face thousands of ordinary situations, which must be met in completely ordinary ways.

God's promises and His providence do not lift us from the world of common sense and everyday trials, for it is through these very things that our faith is perfected. And it is in this world that God loves to interweave the golden threads of His love with the twists and turns of our common, everyday experiences. FROM HARD PLACES IN THE WAY OF FAITH

sorrow and the enlarging of character

Thou hast enlarged me when I was in distress.
(PSALM 4:1 KJV)

This verse is one of the greatest testimonies ever written regarding the effectiveness of God's work on our behalf during times of crisis. It is a statement of thanksgiving for having been set free not *from* suffering but rather *through* suffering. In stating, "Thou hast enlarged me when I was in distress," the psalmist is declaring that the sorrows of life have themselves been the source of life's enlargement.

Haven't each of us experienced this a thousand times and found it to be true? Someone once said of Joseph that when he was in the dungeon, "iron entered his soul." And the strength of iron is exactly what he needed, for earlier he had only experienced the glitter of gold. He had been rejoicing in youthful dreams, and dreaming actually hardens the heart. Someone who sheds great tears over a simple romance will not be of much help in a real crisis, for true sorrow will be too deep for him. We all need the iron in life to enlarge our character. The gold is simply a passing vision, whereas the iron is the true experience of life. The chain that is the common bond uniting us to others must be one of iron. The common touch of humanity that gives the world true kinship is not joy but sorrow—gold is partial to only a few, but iron is universal.

Dear soul, if you want your sympathy for others to be enlarged, you must be willing to have your life narrowed to certain degrees of suffering. Joseph's dungeon was the very road to his throne, and he would have been unable to lift the iron load of his brothers had he not experienced the iron in his own life. Your life will be enlarged in proportion to the amount of iron you have endured, for it is in the shadows of your life that you will find the actual fulfillment of your dreams of glory. So do not complain about the shadows of darkness—in reality, they are better than your dreams could ever be. Do not say that the darkness of the prison has shackled you, for your shackles are wings—wings of flight into the heart and soul of humanity. And the gate of your prison is the gate into the heart of the universe. God has enlarged you through the suffering of sorrow's chain. George Matheson

If Joseph had never been Egypt's prisoner, he would have never been Egypt's governor. The iron chain that bound his feet brought about the golden chain around his neck.

The Divine Mystery in suffering

The LORD will fulfill his purpose for me.
(PSALM 138:8)

There is a divine mystery in suffering, one that has a strange and supernatural power and has never been completely understood by human reason. No one has ever developed a deep level of spirituality or holiness without experiencing a great deal of suffering. When a person who suffers reaches a point where he can be calm and carefree, inwardly smiling at his own suffering, and no longer asking God to be delivered from it, then the suffering has accomplished its blessed ministry, perseverance has "finish[ed] its work" (James 1:4), and the pain of the Crucifixion has begun to weave itself into a crown.

It is in this experience of complete suffering that the Holy Spirit works many miraculous things deep within our soul. In this condition, our entire being lies perfectly still under the hand of God; every power and ability of the mind, will, and heart are at last submissive; a quietness of eternity settles into the entire soul; and finally, the mouth becomes quiet, having only a few words to say, and stops crying out the words Christ quoted on the cross: "My God, my God, why have you forsaken me?" (Ps. 22:1).

At this point the person stops imagining castles in the sky, and pursuing foolish ideas, and his reasoning becomes calm and relaxed, with all choices removed, because the only choice has now become the purpose of God. Also, his emotions are weaned away from other people and things, becoming deadened so that nothing can hurt, offend, hinder, or get in his way. He can now let the circumstances be what they may, and continue to seek only God and His will, with the calm assurance that He is causing everything in the universe, whether good or bad, past or present, to work "for the good of those who love him" (Rom. 8:28).

Oh, the blessings of absolute submission to Christ! What a blessing to lose our own strength, wisdom, plans, and desires and to be where every ounce of our being becomes like a peaceful Sea of Galilee under the omnipotent feet of Jesus!

FROM SOUL FOOD

The main thing is to suffer without becoming discouraged.

FRANÇOIS FÉNELON

The heart that serves, and loves, and clings,
Hears everywhere the rush of angel wings.

suffering, pruning, and abundant fruit

My Father is the gardener.
(JOHN 15:1)

It is a comforting thought that trouble, in whatever form it comes to us, is a heavenly messenger that brings us something from God. Outwardly it may appear painful or even destructive, but inwardly its spiritual work produces blessings. Many of the richest blessings we have inherited are the fruit of sorrow or pain. We should never forget that redemption, the world's greatest blessing, is the fruit of the world's greatest sorrow. And whenever a time of deep pruning comes and the knife cuts deeply and the pain is severe, what an inexpressible comfort it is to know: "My Father is the gardener."

John Vincent, a Methodist Episcopal bishop of the late-nineteenth and early-twentieth centuries and a leader of the Sunday school movement in America, once told of being in a large greenhouse where clusters of luscious grapes were hanging on each side. The owner of the greenhouse told him, "When the new gardener came here, he said he would not work with the vines unless he could cut them completely down to the stalk. I allowed him to do so, and we had no grapes for two years, but this is now the result."

There is rich symbolism in this account of the pruning process when applied to the Christian life. Pruning *seems* to be destroying the vine, and the gardener *appears* to be cutting everything away. Yet he sees the future and knows that the final result will be the enrichment of the life of the vine, and a greater abundance of fruit.

There are many blessings we will never receive until we are ready to pay the price of pain, for the path of suffering is the only way to reach them. J. R. MILLER

I walked a mile with Pleasure,
    She chattered all the way;
But left me none the wiser
    For all she had to say.
I walked a mile with Sorrow,
    And ne'er a word said she;
But oh, the things I learned from her
    When Sorrow walked with me.

adversity and a Higher view of god

The LORD blessed the latter part of Job's life more than the first.

(JOB 42:12)

Job found his legacy through the grief he experienced. He was tried that his godliness might be confirmed and validated. In the same way, my troubles are intended to deepen my character and to clothe me in gifts I had little of prior to my difficulties, for my ripest fruit grows against the roughest wall. I come to a place of glory only through my own humility, tears, and death, just as Job's afflictions left him with a higher view of God and more humble thoughts of himself. At last he cried, *"Now my eyes have seen you"* (v. 5).

If I experience the presence of God in His majesty through my pain and loss, so that I bow before Him and pray, *"Your will be done"* (Matt. 6:10), then I have gained much indeed. God gave Job glimpses of his future glory, for in those weary and difficult days and nights, he was allowed to penetrate God's veil and could honestly say, *"I know that my Redeemer lives"* (Job 19:25). So truly: "The LORD blessed the latter part of Job's life more than the first." FROM IN THE HOUR OF SILENCE

Trouble never comes to someone unless it brings a nugget of gold in its hand.

Apparent adversity will ultimately become an advantage for those of us doing what is right, if we are willing to keep serving and to wait patiently. Think of the great victorious souls of the past who worked with steadfast faith and who were invincible and courageous! There are many blessings we will never obtain if we are unwilling to accept and endure suffering. There are certain joys that can come to us only through sorrow. There are revelations of God's divine truth that we will receive only when the lights of earth have been extinguished. And there are harvests that will grow only once the plow has done its work.

It is from suffering that the strongest souls ever known have emerged; the world's greatest display of character is seen in those who exhibit the scars of sorrow; the martyrs of the ages have worn their coronation robes that have glistened with fire, yet through their tears and sorrow have seen the gates of heaven. CHAPIN

I will know by the gleam and glitter
    Of the golden chain you wear,
By your heart's calm strength in loving,
    Of the fire you have had to bear.
Beat on, true heart, forever;
    Shine bright, strong golden chain;
And bless the cleansing fire
    And the furnace of living pain!

ADELAIDE PROCTOR

The prayer of faith

Jesus replied, "You may go. Your son will live."
The man took Jesus at his word and departed.
(JOHN 4:50)

Whatever you ask for in prayer, believe.
(MARK 11:24)

When you are confronted with a matter that requires immediate prayer, pray until you believe God—until with wholehearted sincerity you can thank Him for the answer. If you do not see the external answer immediately, do not pray for it in such a way that it is evident you are not definitely believing God for it. This type of prayer will be a hindrance instead of a help to you. And when you are finished praying, you will find that your faith has been weakened or has entirely gone. The urgency you felt to offer this kind of prayer is clearly from self and Satan. It may not be wrong to mention the matter to the Lord again, if He is keeping you waiting for His answer, but be sure to do so in a way that shows your faith.

Never pray in a way that diminishes your faith. You may tell Him you are waiting, still believing and therefore praising Him for the answer. There is nothing that so fully solidifies faith as being so sure of the answer that you can thank God for it. Prayers that empty us of faith deny both God's promises from His Word and the "Yes" that He whispered to our hearts. Such prayers are only the expression of the unrest of our hearts, and unrest implies unbelief that our prayers will be answered. "Now we who have believed enter that rest" (Heb. 4:3).

The type of prayer that empties us of faith frequently arises from focusing our thoughts on the difficulty rather than on God's promise. Abraham, "without weakening in his faith,... faced the fact that his body was as good as dead.... Yet he did not waver through unbelief regarding the promise of God, but was strengthened in his faith and gave glory to God" (Rom. 4:19–20). May we "watch and pray so that [we] will not fall into [the] temptation" (Matt. 26:41) of praying faith-diminishing prayers. C. H. P.

Faith is not a sense, nor sight, nor reason, but simply taking God at His word. CHRISTMAS EVANS

The beginning of anxiety is the end of faith, and the beginning of true faith is the end of anxiety. GEORGE MUELLER

You will never learn faith in comfortable surroundings. God gives us His promises in a quiet hour, seals our covenants with great and gracious words, and then steps back, waiting to see how much we believe. He then allows the Tempter to come, and the ensuing test seems to contradict all that He has spoken. This is when faith wins its crown. This is the time to look up through the storm, and among the trembling, frightened sailors declare, "I have faith in God that it will happen just as he told me" (Acts 27:25).

Believe and trust; through stars and suns,
Through life and death, through soul and sense,
His wise, paternal purpose runs;
The darkness of His Providence
Is starlit with Divine intents.

your almighty friend

Then Asa ... said, "LORD, there is no one like you to help the powerless against the mighty."
(2 CHRONICLES 14:11)

Remind God of His exclusive responsibility: "There is no one like you to help." The odds against Asa's men were enormous. "Zerah the Cushite marched out against them with a vast army and three hundred chariots" (v. 9). It seemed impossible for Asa to hold his own against that vast multitude. There were no allies who would come to his defense. Therefore his only hope was in God.

It may be that your difficulties have come to such an alarming level that you may be compelled to refuse all human help. In lesser trials, you may have had that recourse, but now you must cast yourself on your almighty Friend. *Put God between yourself and the enemy.*

Asa, realizing his lack of strength, saw Jehovah as standing between the might of Zerah and himself. And he was not mistaken. We are told that the Cushites "were crushed before the LORD *and his forces*" (v. 13), as though heavenly warriors threw themselves against the enemy on Israel's behalf. God's forces so overwhelmed the vast army of the enemy that they fled. Then all Israel had to do was follow up and gather the plunder. Our God is "the Lord of hosts," who can summon unexpected reinforcements at any moment to help His people. Believe that He is between you and your difficulty, and what troubles you will flee before Him, as clouds in the wind. F. B. MEYER

When nothing on which to lean remains,
  When strongholds crumble to dust;
When nothing is sure but that God still reigns,
  That is just the time to trust.
It's better to walk by faith than sight,
  In this path of yours and mine;
And the darkest night, when there's no outer light
  Is the time for faith to shine.

"Abraham believed God" (Rom. 4:3), and said to his eyes, "Stand back!" and to the laws of nature, "Hold your peace!" and to an unbelieving heart, "Silence, you lying tempter!" He simply "*believed* God." JOSEPH PARKER

passing THROUGH the floodwaters

When you pass through the waters ...
they will not sweep over you.
(ISAIAH 43:2)

God does not open paths for us before we come to them, or provide help before help is needed. He does not remove obstacles out of our way before we reach them. Yet when we are at our point of need, God's hand is outstretched.

Many people forget this truth and continually worry about difficulties they envision in the future. They expect God to open and clear many miles of road before them, but He promises to do it step by step, only as their need arises. You must be in the floodwaters before you can claim God's promise. Many people dread death and are distressed that they do not have "dying grace." Of course, they will never have the grace for death when they are in good health. Why should they have it while in the midst of life's duties, with death still far away? Living grace is what is needed for life's work and calling, and then dying grace when it is time to die.
J. R. M.

"When you pass through the waters"
    Deep the waves may be and cold,
But Jehovah is our refuge,
    And His promise is our hold;
For the Lord Himself has said it,
    He, the faithful God and true:
"When you come to the waters
    You will not go down, but through."
Seas of sorrow, seas of trial,
    Bitter anguish, fiercest pain,
Rolling surges of temptation
    Sweeping over heart and brain—
They will never overflow us
    For we know His word is true;
All His waves and all His billows
    He will lead us safely through.
Threatening breakers of destruction,
    Doubt's insidious undertow,
Will not sink us, will not drag us
    Out to ocean depths of woe;
For His promise will sustain us,
    Praise the Lord, whose Word is true!
We will not go down, or under,
    For He says, "You will pass through."

ANNIE JOHNSON FLINT

without reservation

I have learned to be content whatever the circumstances.
(PHILIPPIANS 4:11)

Paul, while being denied every comfort, wrote the above words from a dark prison cell.

A story is told of a king who went to his garden one morning, only to find everything withered and dying. He asked the oak tree that stood near the gate what the trouble was. The oak said it was tired of life and determined to die because it was not tall and beautiful like the pine tree. The pine was troubled because it could not bear grapes like the grapevine. The grapevine was determined to throw its life away because it could not stand erect and produce fruit as large as peaches. The geranium was fretting because it was not tall and fragrant like the lilac.

And so it went throughout the garden. Yet coming to a violet, the king found its face as bright and happy as ever and said, "Well, violet, I'm glad to find one brave little flower in the midst of this discouragement. You don't seem to be the least disheartened." The violet responded, "No, I'm not. I know I'm small, yet I thought if you wanted an oak or a pine or a peach tree or even a lilac, you would have planted one. Since I knew you wanted a violet, I'm determined to be the best little violet I can be."

Others may do a greater work,
* But you have your part to do;*
And no one in all God's family
* Can do it as well as you.*

 People who are God's without reservation "have learned to be content whatever the circumstances." His will becomes their will, and they desire to do for Him whatever He desires them to do. They strip themselves of everything, and in their nakedness find everything restored a hundredfold.

persist in your calling

Paul and his companions ... [were] kept by the Holy Spirit from preaching the word in the province of Asia.
(ACTS 16:6)

It is interesting to study the way God extended His guidance to these early messengers of the Cross. It consisted mainly in prohibiting their movement when they attempted to take a course other than the right one. When they wanted to turn to the left, toward Asia, He stopped them. When they sought to turn to the right, toward Bithynia in Asia Minor, He stopped them again. In his later years, Paul would do some of his greatest work in that very region, yet now the door was closed before him by the Holy Spirit. The time was not yet ripe for the attack on these apparently impregnable bastions of the kingdom of Satan. Apollos needed to go there first to lay the groundwork. Paul and Barnabas were needed more urgently elsewhere and required further training before undertaking this responsible task.

Beloved, whenever you are in doubt as to which way to turn, submit your judgment absolutely to the Spirit of God, asking Him to shut every door but the right one. Say to Him, "Blessed Spirit, I give to You the entire responsibility of closing every road and stopping every step that is not of God. Let me hear Your voice behind me whenever I 'turn aside to the right or to the left' (Deut. 5:32)."

In the meantime, continue along the path you have already been traveling. Persist in your calling until you are clearly told to do something else. O traveler, the Spirit of Jesus is waiting to be to you what He was to Paul. Just be careful to obey even His smallest nudging or warning. Then after you have prayed the prayer of faith and there are no apparent hindrances, go forward with a confident heart. Do not be surprised if your answer comes in doors closing before you. But when doors are shut to the right and left, an open road is sure to lead to Troas. Luke waits for you there, and visions will point the way to where vast opportunities remain open, and faithful friends are waiting. FROM PAUL, BY F. B. MEYER

Is there some problem in your life to solve,
    Some passage seeming full of mystery?
God knows, who brings the hidden things to light.
        He keeps the key.
Is there some door closed by the Father's hand
    Which widely opened you had hoped to see?
Trust God and wait—for when He shuts the door
        He keeps the key.
Is there some earnest prayer unanswered yet,
    Or answered NOT as you had thought 'twould be?
God will make clear His purpose by and by.
        He keeps the key.
Have patience with your God, your patient God,
    All wise, all knowing, no long lingerer He,
And of the door of all your future life
        He keeps the key.
Unfailing comfort, sweet and blessed rest,
    To know of EVERY door He keeps the key.
That He at last when just HE sees is best,
        Will give it THEE.

ANONYMOUS

This is my doing

This is my doing.
(1 KINGS 12:24)

The disappointments of life are simply the hidden appointments of love. C. A. Fox

My child, I have a message for you today. Let Me whisper it in your ear so any storm clouds that may arise will shine with glory, and the rough places you may have to walk will be made smooth. It is only four words, but let them sink into your inner being, and use them as a pillow to rest your weary head. *"This is* my *doing."*

Have you ever realized that whatever concerns you concerns Me too? "For whoever touches you touches the apple of [my] eye" (Zech. 2:8). "You are precious and honored in my sight" (Isa. 43:4). Therefore it is My special delight to teach you.

I want you to learn when temptations attack you, and the enemy comes in "like a pent-up flood" (Isa. 59:19), that *"this is* my *doing"* and that your weakness needs My strength, and your safety lies in letting Me fight for you.

Are you in difficult circumstances, surrounded by people who do not understand you, never ask your opinion, and always push you aside? *"This is* my *doing."* I am the God of circumstances. You did not come to this place by accident—you are exactly where I meant for you to be.

Have you not asked Me to make you humble? Then see that I have placed you in the perfect school where this lesson is taught. Your circumstances and the people around you are only being used to accomplish My will.

Are you having problems with money, finding it hard to make ends meet? *"This is* my *doing,"* for I am the One who keeps your finances, and I want you to learn to depend upon Me. My supply is limitless and I "will meet all your needs" (Phil. 4:19). I want you to prove My promises so no one may say, "You did not trust in the LORD your God" (Deut. 1:32).

Are you experiencing a time of sorrow? *"This is* my *doing."* I am "a man of sorrows, and familiar with suffering" (Isa. 53:3). I have allowed your earthly comforters to fail you, so that by turning to Me you may receive "eternal encouragement and good hope" (2 Thess. 2:16). Have you longed to do some great work for Me but instead have been set aside on a bed of sickness and pain? *"This is* my *doing."* You were so busy I could not get your attention, and I wanted to teach you some of My deepest truths. "They also serve who only stand and wait." In fact, some of My greatest workers are those physically unable to serve, but who have learned to wield the powerful weapon of prayer.

Today I place a cup of holy oil in your hands. Use it freely, My child. Anoint with it every new circumstance, every word that hurts you, every interruption that makes you impatient, and every weakness you have. The pain will leave as you learn to see Me in all things. Laura A. Barter Snow

"This is from Me," the Savior said,
	As bending low He kissed my brow,
"For One who loves you thus has led.
	Just rest in Me, be patient now,
Your Father knows you have need of this,
	Though, why perhaps you cannot see—
Grieve not for things you've seemed to miss.
	The thing I send is best for thee."
Then, looking through my tears, I plead,
	"Dear Lord, forgive, I did not know,
It will not be hard since You do tread
	Each path before me here below."
And for my good this thing must be,
	His grace sufficient for each test.
So still I'll sing, "Whatever be
	God's way for me is always best."

in the shadow of god's hand

In the shadow of his hand he hid me; he made me into a polished arrow and concealed me in his quiver.
(ISAIAH 49:2)

"In the shadow"— each of us must go there sometimes. The glare of the sunlight is too bright, and our eyes become injured. Soon they are unable to discern the subtle shades of

color or appreciate neutral tints, such as the shadowed sickroom, the shadowed house of grief, or the shadowed life where the sunlight has departed.

But fear not! It is the shadow of God's hand. He is leading you, and there are lessons that can be learned only where He leads.

The photograph of His face can only be developed in the dark room. But do not assume that He has pushed you aside. You are still "in his quiver." He has not thrown you away as something worthless.

He is only keeping you nearby till the moment comes when He can send you quickly and confidently on some mission that will bring Him glory. O shadowed, isolated one, remember how closely the quiver is tied to the warrior. It is always within easy reach of his hand and jealously protected.

FROM CHRIST IN ISAIAH, BY F. B. MEYER

In some realms of nature, shadows or darkness are the places of greatest growth. The beautiful Indian corn never grows more rapidly than in the darkness of a warm summer night. The sun withers and curls the leaves in the scorching light of noon, but once a cloud hides the sun, they quickly unfold. The shadows provide a service that the sunlight does not. The starry beauty of the sky cannot be seen at its peak until the shadows of night slip over the sky. Lands with fog, clouds, and shade are lush with greenery. And there are beautiful flowers that bloom in the shade that will never bloom in the sun. Florists now have their evening primrose as well as their morning glory. The evening primrose will not open in the noonday sun but only reveals its beauty as the shadows of the evening grow longer.

If all of life were sunshine,
*   Our face would long to gain*
And feel once more upon it
*   The cooling splash of rain.*

HENRY JACKSON VAN DYKE

god will Deliver you

Consider what God has done: Who can straighten what he has made crooked?
(ECCLESIASTES 7:13)

God often seems to place His children in places of deep difficulty, leading them into a corner from which there is no escape. He creates situations that human judgment, even if consulted, would never allow. Yet the cloudiness of the circumstance itself is used by Him to guide us to the other side. Perhaps this is where you find yourself even now.

Your situation is filled with uncertainty and is very serious, but it is perfectly right. The reason behind it will more than justify Him who brought you here, for it is a platform from which God will display His almighty grace and power.

He not only will deliver you but in doing so will impart a lesson that you will never forget. And in days to come, you will return to the truth of it through singing. You will be unable to ever thank God enough for doing exactly what He has done.

We may wait till He explains,
Because we know that Jesus reigns.
It puzzles me; but, Lord, You understandest,
*   And will one day explain this crooked thing.*
Meanwhile, I know that it has worked out Your best—
*   Its very crookedness taught me to cling.*
You have fenced up my ways, made my paths crooked,
*   To keep my wand'ring eyes fixed on You,*
To make me what I was not, humble, patient;
*   To draw my heart from earthly love to You.*
So I will thank and praise You for this puzzle,
*   And trust where I cannot understand.*
Rejoicing You do hold me worth such testing,
*   I cling the closer to Your guiding hand.*

F. E. M. I.

trials—god's school of faith

We were harassed at every turn.
(2 CORINTHIANS 7:5)

Why is it that God leads us in this way, allowing such strong and constant pressure on us? One of His purposes is to show us His all-sufficient strength and grace more effectively than if we were free from difficulties and trials. "We have this treasure in jars of clay to show that this all-surpassing power is from God and not from us" (2 Cor. 4:7).

Another purpose is to bring us a greater awareness of our dependence upon Him. God is constantly trying to teach us how dependent we are on Him—that we are held completely by His hand and reliant on His care alone.

This is exactly where Jesus Himself stood and where He desires us to stand. We must stand not with self-made strength but always leaning upon Him. And our stand must exhibit a trust that would never dare to take even one step alone. This will teach us to trust Him more.

There is no way to learn of faith except through trials. They are God's school of faith, and it is much better for us to learn to trust Him than to live a life of enjoyment. And once the lesson of faith has been learned, it is an everlasting possession and an eternal fortune gained. Yet without trust in God, even great riches will leave us in poverty. FROM DAYS OF HEAVEN UPON EARTH

Why must I weep when others sing?
  "To test the deeps of suffering."
Why must I work while others rest?
  "To spend my strength at God's request."
Why must I lose while others gain?
  "To understand defeat's sharp pain."
Why must this lot of life be mine
When that which fairer seems is thine?
  "Because God knows what plans for me
    Will blossom in eternity."

great and precious promises

Do as you promised ... that your name
will be great forever.
(1 CHRONICLES 17:23–24)

This is one of the most blessed aspects of genuine prayer. Often we ask for things that God has not specifically promised. Therefore we are not sure if our petitions are in line with His purpose, until we have persevered for some time in prayer. Yet on some occasions, and this was one in the life of David, we are fully persuaded that what we are asking is in accordance with God's will. We feel led to select and plead a promise from the pages of Scripture, having been specially impressed that it contains a message for us. At these times, we may say with confident faith, "Do as you promised."

Hardly any stance could be more completely beautiful, strong, or safe than that of putting your finger on a promise of God's divine Word and then claiming it. Doing so requires no anguish, struggle, or wrestling but simply presenting the check and asking for cash. It is as simple as producing the promise and claiming its fulfillment. Nor will there be any doubt or cloudiness about the request. If all requests were this definitive, there would be much more interest in prayer. It is much better to claim a few specific things than to make twenty vague requests. F. B. Meyer

Every promise of Scripture is a letter from God, which we may plead before Him with this reasonable request: *"Do as you promised."* Our Creator will never cheat those of us of His creation who depend upon His truth. And even more, our heavenly Father will never break His word to His own child.

"Remember your word to your servant, for you have given me hope" (Ps. 119:49). This is a very common plea and is a double argument, for it is "your *word*." Will You not keep it? Why have You spoken it, if You will not make it good? "You have given me hope." Will You now disappoint the hope that You Yourself have brought forth within me? Charles H. Spurgeon

He did not waver through unbelief regarding the promise of God, but was strengthened in his faith and gave glory to God, being fully persuaded that God had power to do what he had promised (Romans 4:20–21).

It is the everlasting faithfulness of God that makes a Bible promise "very great and precious" (2 Peter 1:4). Human promises are often worthless, and many broken promises have left broken hearts. But since the creation of the world, God has never broken a single promise to one of His trusting children.

Oh, how sad it is for a poor Christian to stand at the very door of a promise during a dark night of affliction, being afraid to turn the knob and thereby come boldly into the shelter as a child entering his Father's house! Gurnal

Every promise of God's is built on four pillars. The first two are His justice and holiness, which will never allow Him to deceive us. The third is His grace or goodness, which will not allow Him to forget. And the fourth is His truth, which will not allow Him to change, which enables Him to accomplish what He has promised.

the fact of god's faithfulness

My righteous one will live by faith.
(HEBREWS 10:38)

Often our feelings and emotions are mistakenly substituted for faith. Pleasurable emotions and deep, satisfying experiences are part of the Christian life, but they are not the essence of it. Trials, conflicts, battles, and testings lie along the way and are to be counted not as misfortunes but rather as part of our necessary discipline.

In all of these various experiences, we are to rely on the indwelling of Christ in our hearts, regardless of our feelings, as we walk obediently before Him. And this is where many Christians get into trouble. They try to walk by feelings rather than by faith.

A believer once related that it seemed as if God had totally withdrawn Himself from her. His mercy *seemed* completely gone. Her loneliness lasted for six weeks, until the heavenly Lover seemed to say to her, "You have looked for Me in the outside world of emotions, yet all the while I have been waiting inside for you. Meet Me now in the inner chamber of your spirit, *for I am there.*"

Be sure to distinguish between the fact of God's presence and the *feeling* of the fact. It is actually a wonderful thing when our soul feels lonely and deserted, as long as our faith can say,

"I do not see You, Lord, nor do I feel Your presence, but I know for certain You are graciously here—exactly where I am and aware of my circumstances." Remind yourself again and again with these words: "Lord, You are here. And though the bush before me does not seem to burn, it *does* burn. I will take the shoes from my feet, 'for the place where [I am] standing is holy ground'" (Ex. 3:5). London Christian

Trust God's Word and His power more than you trust your own feelings and experiences. Remember, your Rock is Christ, and it is the sea that ebbs and flows with the tides, not Him. Samuel Rutherford

Keep your eyes firmly fixed on the infinite greatness of Christ's finished work and His righteousness. Look to Jesus and believe—look to Jesus and live! In fact, as you look to Him, unfurl your sails and bravely face the raging storms on the sea of life. Do not exhibit your distrust by staying in the security of the calm harbor or by sleeping comfortably through your life of ease. Do not allow your life and emotions to be tossed back and forth against each other like ships idly moored at port. The Christian life is not one of listless brooding over our emotions or slowly drifting our keel of faith through shallow water. Nor is it one of dragging our anchor of

hope through the settling mud of the bay, as if we were afraid of encountering a healthy breeze.

Sail away! Spread your sail toward the storm and trust in Him who rules the raging seas. A brightly colored bird is safest when in flight. If its nest is near the ground or if it flies too low, it exposes itself to the hunter's net or trap. In the same way, if we cower in the lowlands of feelings and emotions, we will find ourselves entangled in a thousand nets of doubt, despair, temptation, and unbelief. "How useless to spread a net in full view of ALL THE BIRDS!" (Prov. 1:17). "Put your hope in God" (Ps. 42:5). J. R. MACDUFF

When I cannot *feel* the faith of assurance, I live by the *fact* of God's faithfulness. MATTHEW HENRY

A steadfast Anchor

Though he slay me, yet will I hope in him.
(JOB 13:15)

Because I know whom I have believed.
(2 TIMOTHY 1:12)

I will not doubt, though all my ships at sea
   Come drifting home with broken masts and sails;
   I will believe the Hand that never fails,

From seeming evil works to good for me.
    And though I weep because those sails are tattered,
    Still will I cry, while my best hopes lie shattered:
        "I trust in Thee."
I will not doubt, though all my prayers return
    Unanswered from the still, white realm above;
    I will believe it is an all-wise love
That has refused these things for which I yearn;
    And though at times I cannot keep from grieving,
    Yet the pure passion of my fixed believing
        Undimmed will burn.
I will not doubt, though sorrows fall like rain,
    And troubles swarm like bees about a hive.
    I will believe the heights for which I strive
Are only reached by anguish and by pain;
    And though I groan and writhe beneath my crosses,
    Yet I will see through my severest losses
        The greater gain.
I will not doubt. Well anchored is this faith,
    Like some staunch ship, my soul braves every gale;
    So strong its courage that it will not fail
To face the mighty unknown sea of death.
    Oh, may I cry, though body leaves the spirit,
    "I do not doubt," so listening worlds may hear it,
        With my last breath.

An old seaman once said, "In fierce storms we must do one thing, for there is only one way to survive: we must put the ship in a certain position and keep her there." And this, dear Christian, is what you must do.

Sometimes, like Paul, you cannot see the sun or the stars to help you navigate when the storm is bearing down on you. This is when you can do only one thing, for there is only one way. Reason cannot help you, past experiences will shed no light, and even prayer will bring no consolation. Only one course remains: you must put your soul in one position and keep it there.

You must anchor yourself steadfastly upon the Lord. And then, come what may—whether wind, waves, rough seas, thunder, lightning, jagged rocks, or roaring breakers—you must lash yourself to the helm, firmly holding your confidence in God's faithfulness, His covenant promises, and His everlasting love in Christ Jesus. RICHARD FULLER

keep looking up!

They looked ... and there was the glory of the LORD appearing in the cloud.
(EXODUS 16:10)

You should get into the habit of looking for the silver lining of storm clouds. And once you have found it, continue to focus on it rather than the dark gray of the center. Do not yield to discouragement no matter how severely stressed or surrounded by problems you may be. A discouraged soul is in a helpless state, being neither able to "stand against the devil's schemes" (Eph. 6:11) himself nor able to prevail in prayer for others. Flee every symptom of the deadly foe of discouragement as you would run from a snake. Never be slow to turn your back on it, unless you desire to eat the dust of bitter defeat.

Search for specific promises of God, saying aloud of each one, "This promise is *mine*." Then if you still experience feelings of doubt and discouragement, pour your heart out to God, asking Him to rebuke the Adversary who is so mercilessly harassing you.

The very instant you wholeheartedly turn away from every symptom of discouragement and lack of trust, the blessed Holy Spirit will reawaken your faith and breathe God's divine strength into your soul. Initially you may be unaware that this is happening, but as you determine to uncompromisingly *shun* every attack of even the tendency toward doubt and depression, you will quickly see the powers of darkness being turned back.

Oh, if only our eyes could see the mighty armies of strength and power that are always behind our turning away from the hosts of darkness toward God, there would be no attention given to the efforts of our cunning Foe to distress, depress, or discourage us! All the miraculous attributes of the Godhead are marshaled on the side of even the weakest believer who, in the name of Christ and in simple, childlike trust, yields himself to God and turns to Him for help and guidance.

One day in autumn, while on the open prairie, I saw an eagle mortally wounded by a rifle shot. With his eyes still gleaming like small circles of light, he slowly turned his head, giving one last searching and longing look toward the sky. He had often swept those starry spaces with his wonderful wings. The beautiful sky was the home of his heart. It was the eagle's domain. It was there he had displayed his splendid strength a thousand times. In those lofty heights, he had played with the lightning and raced the wind. And now, far below his home, the eagle lay dying. He faced death because—just once—he forgot and flew too low.

My soul is that eagle. This is not its home. It must never lose its skyward look. I must keep faith, I must keep hope, I must keep courage, I must keep Christ. It would be better to crawl immediately from the battlefield than to not be brave. There is no time for my soul to retreat. Keep your skyward look, my soul; keep your skyward look!

Keep looking up—
The waves that roar around your feet,
Jehovah-Jireh will defeat
When looking up.
Keep looking up—
Though darkness seems to wrap your soul;

The Light of Light will fill your soul
  When looking up.
  Keep looking up—
When worn, distracted with the fight;
Your Captain gives you conquering might
  When you look up.

We can never see the sunrise by looking toward the west.

JAPANESE PROVERB

from promise to prophecy

God, who does not lie, promised.
(TITUS 1:2)

Faith is not conjuring up, through an act of your will, a sense of certainty that something is going to happen. No, it is recognizing God's promise as an actual fact, believing it is true, rejoicing in the knowledge of that truth, and then simply resting because God said it.

Faith turns a promise into a prophecy. A promise is contingent upon our cooperation, but when we exercise genuine faith in it, it becomes a prophecy. Then we can move ahead with certainty that it will come to pass, because "God ... does not lie." FROM DAYS OF HEAVEN UPON EARTH

I often hear people praying for more faith, but when I listen carefully to them and get to the essence of their prayer, I realize it is not more faith they are wanting at all. What they are wanting is their faith to be changed to sight.

Faith does not say, "I see this is good for me; therefore God must have sent it." Instead, faith declares, "God sent it; therefore it must be good for me."

Faith, when walking through the dark with God, only asks Him to hold his hand more tightly. PHILLIPS BROOKS

The Shepherd does not ask of thee
*   Faith in your faith, but only faith in Him;*
And this He meant in saying, "Come to me."
*   In light or darkness seek to do His will,*
*   And leave the work of faith to Jesus still.*

Run to the Living God

Everyone who calls on the name of the LORD
will be saved.
(JOEL 2:32)

So why don't I call on His name? Why do I run to this person or that person, when God is so near and will hear my faintest call? Why do I sit down to plot my own course and make my own plans? Why don't I immediately place myself and my burden on the Lord?

Straight ahead is the best way to run, so why don't I run directly to the living God? Instead, I look in vain for deliverance everywhere else, but with God I will find it. With Him I have His royal promise: "[I] *will* be saved." And with Him I never need to ask if I may call on Him or not, for the word "everyone" is all encompassing. It includes me and means anybody and everybody who calls upon His name. Therefore I will trust in this verse and will immediately call on the glorious Lord who has made such a great promise.

My situation is urgent, and I cannot see how I will ever be delivered. Yet this is not my concern, for He who made the promise will find a way to keep it. My part is simply to obey His commands, not to direct His ways. I am His servant, not His advisor. I call upon Him and He will deliver me.

CHARLES H. SPURGEON

The Appointed Time

Sarah became pregnant and bore a son to Abraham in his old age, at the very time God had promised him.
(GENESIS 21:2)

The plans of the LORD stand firm forever, the purposes of his heart through all generations" (Ps. 33:11). But we must be prepared to wait on God's timing. His timing is precise, for He does things "at the very time" He has set. It is not for us to know His timing, and in fact we cannot know it—we must wait for it.

If God had told Abraham while he was in Haran that he would have to wait thirty years before holding his promised child in his arms, his heart might have failed him. So God, as an act of His gracious love, hid from Abraham the number of weary years he would be required to wait. Only as the time was approaching, with but a few months left to wait, did God reveal His promise: "At the appointed time next year ... Sarah will have a son" (Gen. 18:14). The "appointed time" came at last, and soon the joyous laughter that filled the patriarch's home caused the now elderly couple to forget their long and tiring wait.

So take heart, dear child, when God requires you to wait. The One you wait for will not disappoint you. He will never be even five minutes behind "the appointed time." And soon "your grief will turn to joy" (John 16:20).

Oh, how joyful the soul that God brings to laughter! Then sorrow and crying flee forever, as darkness flees the dawn.

As passengers, it is not for us to interfere with the charts and the compass. We should leave the masterful Captain alone to do His own work. ROBERT HALL

Some things cannot be accomplished in a day. Even God does not make a glorious sunset in a moment. For several days He gathers the mist with which to build His beautiful palaces in the western sky.

Some glorious morn—but when? Ah, who will say?
The steepest mountain will become a plain,
And the parched land be satisfied with rain.
The gates of brass all broken; iron bars,
Transfigured, form a ladder to the stars.
Rough places plain, and crooked ways all straight,
For him who with a patient heart can wait.
These things will be on God's appointed day:
It may not be tomorrow—yet it may.

Hands off!

We do not know what to do, but our eyes are upon you.
(2 CHRONICLES 20:12)

An Israelite named Uzzah lost his life because he "reached out and took hold of the ark of God" (2 Sam. 6:6). He placed his hands on it with the best of intentions—to steady it, "because the oxen stumbled" (2 Sam. 6:6)—but nevertheless, he had overstepped his bounds by touching the Lord's work, and "therefore God struck him down" (2 Sam. 6:7). *Living a life of faith often requires us to leave things alone.*

If we have completely entrusted something to God, we must keep our hands off it. He can guard it better than we can, and He does not need our help. "Be still before the LORD and wait patiently for him; do not fret when men succeed in their ways, when they carry out their wicked schemes" (Ps. 37:7).

Things in our lives may seem to be going all wrong, but God knows our circumstances better than we do. And He will work at the perfect moment, if we will completely trust Him to work in His own way and in His own time. Often there is nothing as godly as inactivity on our part, or nothing as harmful as restless working, for God has promised to work His sovereign will. A. B. SIMPSON

Being perplexed, I say,
    "Lord, make it right!
Night is as day to You,
    Darkness as light.
I am afraid to touch
Things that involve so much;
My trembling hand may shake,
My skilless hand may break;
Yours can make no mistake."
Being in doubt I say,

"Lord, make it plain;
Which is the true, safe way?
Which would be gain?
I am not wise to know,
Nor sure of foot to go;
What is so clear to Thee,
Lord, make it clear to me!"

It is such a comfort to drop the entanglements and perplexities of life into God's hands and leave them there.

stepping out in faith

God ... calls things that are not as though they were.
(ROMANS 4:17)

What does this verse mean? It is the very reason why "Abraham in hope believed" (v. 18). That Abraham would become the father of a child at his advanced age seemed absurd and an utter impossibility, yet God called him "the father of many nations" (Gen. 17:4) long before there was any indication of fulfillment. And Abraham thought of himself as a father, because God had said so. That is genuine faith—believing and declaring what God has said, stepping out on what appears to be thin air and finding solid rock beneath your feet.

Therefore boldly declare what God says you have, and He will accomplish what you believe. You must, however, exhibit genuine faith and trust Him with your entire being.
FROM CRUMBS

We must be willing to live by faith, not hoping or desiring to live any other way. We must be willing to have every light around us extinguished, to have every star in the heavens

blotted out, and to live with nothing encircling us but darkness and danger. Yes, we must be willing to do all this, if God will only leave within our soul an inner radiance from the pure, bright light that faith has kindled. THOMAS C. UPHAM

The moment has come when you must jump from your perch of distrust, leaving the nest of supposed safety behind and trusting the wings of faith. You must be like a young bird beginning to test the air with its untried wings. At first you may feel as though you will fall to the earth. The fledgling may feel the same way, but it does not fall, for its wings provide support. Yet even if its wings do fail, one of its parents will sweep under it, rescuing it on strong wings.

God will rescue you in the same way. Simply trust Him, for His "right hand sustains" (Ps. 18:35). Do you find yourself asking, "But am I to step out onto nothing?" That is exactly what the bird is seemingly asked to do, yet we know that the *air is there* and that the air is not nearly as insubstantial as it seems. And *you* know that the *promises of God are there,* and they certainly are not insubstantial at all. Do you still respond, "But it seems so unlikely that my poor, helpless soul would be sustained by such strength." Has God said it will? "Do you mean that my tempted, yielding nature will be victorious in the fight?" Has God said it will? "Do you mean that my timid, trembling heart will find peace?" Has God said it will?

If God has said so, surely you do not want to suggest He has lied! If He has spoken, will He not fulfill it? If He has given you His word—His sure word of promise—do not question it but trust it absolutely. You have His promise, and in fact you have even more—you have Him who confidently speaks the words.

"Yes, I tell you" (Luke 12:5). Trust Him! J. B. FIGGIS

Genuine Faith Indeed

This is the victory that has overcome the world, even our faith.

(1 JOHN 5:4)

It is easy to love Him when the blue is in the sky,
When the summer winds are blowing, and we smell
*   the roses nigh;*
There is little effort needed to obey His precious will
When it leads through flower-decked valley, or over
*   sun-kissed hill.*
It is when the rain is falling, or the mist hangs in the air,
When the road is dark and rugged, and the wind no
*   longer fair,*
When the rosy dawn has settled in a shadowland of gray,
That we find it hard to trust Him, and are slower to obey.
It is easy to trust Him when the singing birds have come,

And their songs of praise are echoed in our heart and
    in our home;
But it's when we miss the music, and the days are
    dull and drear,
That we need a faith triumphant over every doubt
    and fear.
And our blessed Lord will give it; what we lack He
    will supply;
Let us ask in faith believing—on His promises rely;
He will ever be our Leader, whether smooth or rough
    the way,
And will prove Himself sufficient for the needs of
    every day.

Trusting even when it appears you have been forsaken; praying when it seems your words are simply entering a vast expanse where no one hears and no voice answers; believing that God's love is complete and that He is aware of your circumstances, even when your world seems to grind on as if setting its own direction and not caring for life or moving one inch in response to your petitions; desiring only what God's hands have planned for you; waiting patiently while seemingly starving to death, with your only fear being that your faith might fail— "this is the victory that has overcome the world"; this is genuine faith indeed. GEORGE MACDONALD

my grace is sufficient

My grace is sufficient for you.
(2 CORINTHIANS 12:9)

"God was pleased" (1 Cor. 1:21) to take my youngest child from this world, under circumstances that caused me severe trials and pain. And as I returned home from the church cemetery, having just laid my little one's body in the grave, I felt a compulsion to preach to my people on the meaning of trials.

I found that the verse "My grace is sufficient for you" was the text of next week's Sunday school lesson, so I chose it as my Master's message to the congregation, as well as His message to me. Yet while trying to write the sermon, I found that in all honesty, I could not say that the words were true in my life. Therefore I knelt down and asked the Lord to make His grace sufficient for me. While I was pleading in this way, I opened my eyes and saw this exact verse framed and hanging on the wall. My mother had given it to me a few days before, when I was still at the vacation resort where our little child had been taken from us. I had asked someone to hang it on the wall at home during my absence but had not yet noticed its words. Now as I looked up and wiped my eyes, the words met my gaze: "My grace *is* sufficient for you."

The word "is" was highlighted in bright green, while the words "my" and "you" were painted in yet another color. In a moment, a message flashed straight to my soul, coming as a rebuke for having prayed such a prayer as, "Lord, make Your grace sufficient for me." His answer was almost an audible voice that said, "How dare you ask for something that is? I cannot make My grace any more sufficient than I have already made it. Get up and believe it, and you will find it to be true in your life."

The Lord says it in the simplest way: "My grace is [not will be or may be] sufficient for you." The words "my," "is," and "you" were from that moment indelibly written upon my heart. And thankfully, I have been trying to live in the reality of that truth from that day to the present time.

The underlying lesson that came to me through this experience, and that I seek to convey to others, is this: *Never change God's facts into hopes or prayers but simply accept them as realities, and you will find them to be powerful as you believe them.* H. W. WEBB PEPLOE

He giveth more grace when the burdens grow greater,
He sendeth more strength when the labors increase;
To added affliction He addeth His mercies,
To multiplied trials His multiplied peace.
When we have exhausted our store of endurance,
When our strength has failed ere the day is half done,
When we reach the end of our hoarded resources
Our Father's full giving is only begun.

His love has no limit, His grace has no measure,
His power no boundary known unto men;
For out of His infinite riches in Jesus
He giveth and giveth and giveth again.

ANNIE JOHNSON FLINT

Lessons Learned Through Tears

It has been granted to you ... to suffer for him.
(PHILIPPIANS 1:29)

God runs a costly school, for many of His lessons are learned through tears. Richard Baxter, the seventeenth-century Puritan preacher, once said, "O God, I thank You for the discipline I have endured in this body for fifty-eight years." And he certainly is not the only person who has turned trouble into triumph.

Soon the school of our heavenly Father will close for us, for the end of the school term is closer every day. May we never run from a difficult lesson or flinch from the rod of discipline. Richer will be our crown, and sweeter will heaven be, if we cheerfully endure to the end. Then we will graduate in glory. THEODORE L. CUYLER

The world's finest china is fired in ovens at least three times, and some many more. Dresden china is always fired three times. *Why* is it forced to endure such intense heat? Shouldn't once or twice be enough? No, it is necessary to fire the china three times so the gold, crimson, and other colors are brighter, more beautiful, and permanently attached.

We are fashioned after the same principle. The human trials of life are burned into us numerous times, and through God's grace, beautiful colors are formed in us and made to shine forever. CORTLAND MYERS

Earth's fairest flowers grow not on sunny plain,
But where some vast upheaval tore in twain
The smiling land.
After the whirlwind's devastating blast,
And molten lava, fire, and ashes fall,
God's still small voice breathes healing over all.
From broken rocks and fern-clad chasms deep,
Flow living waters as from hearts that weep,
There in the afterglow soft dews distill
And angels tend God's plants when night falls still,
And the Beloved passing by the way
Will gather lilies at the break of day.

J. H. D.

HE IS WITH US IN TROUBLE

God is our refuge and strength, an ever-present help in trouble.

(PSALM 46:1)

Why didn't God help me sooner?" This is a question that is often asked, but it is not His will to act on *your* schedule. He desires to change you through the trouble and cause you to learn a lesson from it. He has promised, "I will be with him *in* trouble, I will deliver him and honor him" (Ps. 91:15). He will be with you *in* trouble all day and through the night. Afterward he will take you out of it, but not until you have stopped being restless and worried over it and have become calm and quiet. Then He will say, "It is enough."

God uses trouble to teach His children precious lessons. Difficulties are intended to educate us, and when their good work is done, a glorious reward will become ours through them. There is a sweet joy and a real value in difficulties, for He regards them not as difficulties but as opportunities.

Not always OUT of our troubled times,
*   And the struggles fierce and grim,*
But in—deeper in—to our sure rest,
*   The place of our peace, in Him.*

ANNIE JOHNSON FLINT

I once heard the following statement from a simple old man, and I have never forgotten it: "When God tests you, it is a good time to test Him by putting His promises to the test and then claiming from Him exactly what your trials have made necessary."

There are two ways of getting out of a trial. One is simply to try to get rid of the trial, and then to be thankful when it is over. The other is to recognize the trial as a challenge from God to claim a larger blessing than we have ever before experienced, and to accept it with delight as an opportunity of receiving a greater measure of God's divine grace.

In this way, even the Adversary becomes a help to us, and all the things that seem to be against us turn out to assist us along our way. Surely this is what is meant by the words "In all these things we are more than conquerors through him who loved us" (Rom. 8:37). A. B. Simpson

The Blessings of Solitude

He took them with him and they withdrew by themselves.
(LUKE 9:10)

In order to grow in grace, we must spend a great deal of time in quiet solitude. Contact with others in society is not what causes the soul to grow most vigorously. In fact, one quiet hour of prayer will often yield greater results than many days spent in the company of others. It is in the desert that the dew is freshest and the air is the most pure. ANDREW BONAR

Come with me by yourselves and rest awhile;
    I know you're weary of the stress and throng.
Wipe from your brow the sweat and dust of toil,
    And in My quiet strength again be strong.
Come now aside from all the world holds dear,
    For fellowship the world has never known,
Alone with Me, and with My Father here,
    With Me and with My Father, not alone.
Come, tell Me all that you have said and done,
    Your victories and failures, hopes and fears.
I know how hardened hearts are wooed and won;
    My choicest wreaths are always wet with tears.
Come now and rest; the journey is too great,
    And you will faint beside the way and sink;
The bread of life is here for you to eat,
    And here for you the wine of love to drink.
Then from fellowship with your Lord return,
    And work till daylight softens into even:
Those brief hours are not lost in which you learn
    More of your Master and His rest in Heaven.

mind the checks

After the earthquake came a fire....
And after the fire came a gentle whisper.
(1 KINGS 19:12)

A woman who had made rapid progress in her understanding of the Lord was once asked the secret of her seemingly easy growth. Her brief response was, *"Mind the checks."*

The reason many of us do not know and understand God better is that we do not heed His gentle "checks"—His delicate restraints and constraints. His voice is "a gentle whisper." A whisper can hardly be heard, so it must be felt as a faint and steady pressure upon the heart and mind, like the touch of a morning breeze calmly moving across the soul. And when it is heeded, it quietly grows clearer in the inner ear of the heart.

God's voice is directed to the ear of love, and true love is intent upon hearing even the faintest whisper. Yet there comes a time when His love ceases to speak, when we do not respond to or believe His message. "God is love" (1 John 4:8), and if you want to know Him and His voice, you must continually listen to His gentle touches.

So when you are about to say something in conversation with others, and you sense a gentle restraint from His quiet whisper, heed the restraint and refrain from speaking. And when you are about to pursue some course of action that seems perfectly clear and right, yet you sense in your spirit another path being suggested with the force of quiet conviction, heed that conviction. Follow the alternate course, even if the change of plans appears to be absolute folly from the perspective of human wisdom.

Also learn to wait on God until He unfolds His will before you. Allow Him to develop all the plans of your heart and mind, and then let Him accomplish them. Do not possess any wisdom of your own, for often His performance will appear to contradict the plan He gave you. God will seem to work against Himself, so simply listen, obey, and trust Him, even when it appears to be the greatest absurdity to do so. Ultimately, "we know that in all things God works for the good of those who love him" (Rom. 8:28), but many times, in the initial stages of the performance of His plans:

In His own world He is content
  To play a losing game.

Therefore if you desire to know God's voice, never consider the final outcome or the possible results. Obey Him even when He asks you to move while you still see only darkness, for He Himself will be a glorious light within you. Then there will quickly spring up within your heart a knowledge of God and a fellowship with Him, which will be overpowering enough in themselves to hold you and Him together, even in the most severe tests and under the strongest pressures of life. FROM WAY OF FAITH

The only thing "too hard for the lord"

Is anything too hard for the LORD?
(GENESIS 18:14)

This is God's loving challenge to you and me each day. He wants us to think of the deepest, highest, and worthiest desires and longings of our hearts. He wants us to think of those things that perhaps were desires for ourselves or someone dear to us, yet have gone unfulfilled for so long that we now see them as simply lost desires. And God urges us to think of even the one thing that we once saw as possible but have given up all hope of seeing fulfilled in this life.

That very thing, as long as it aligns with what we know to be His expressed will—as a son was to Abraham and Sarah—God intends to *do* for us. Yes, if we will let Him, God will do *that very thing,* even if we know it is such an utter impossibility that we would simply laugh at the absurdity of anyone ever suggesting it could come to pass.

"Is anything too hard for the LORD?" No, nothing is too difficult when we believe in Him enough to go forward,

doing His will and letting Him do the impossible for us. Even Abraham and Sarah could have blocked God's plan if they had continued to disbelieve.

The only thing "too hard for the LORD" is our deliberate and continual disbelief in His love and power, and our ultimate rejection of His plans for us. Nothing is impossible for Jehovah to do for those who trust Him. FROM MESSAGES FOR THE MORNING WATCH

The Arrows of God

Those whom I love I rebuke and discipline.
(REVELATION 3:19)

God selects the best and most notable of His servants for the best and most notable afflictions, for those who have received the most grace from Him are able to endure the most afflictions. In fact, an affliction hits a believer never by chance but by God's divine direction. He does not haphazardly aim His arrows, for each one is on a special mission and touches only the heart for whom it is intended. It is not only the grace of God but also His glory that is revealed when a believer can stand and quietly endure an affliction. JOSEPH CARYL

If all my days were sunny, could I say,
"In His fair land He wipes all tears away"?
If I were never weary, could I keep
This blessed truth, "He gives His loved ones sleep"?
If no grave were mine, I might come to deem
The Life Eternal but a baseless dream.
My winter, and my tears, and weariness,
Even my grave, may be His way to bless.
I call them ills; yet that can surely be
Nothing but love that shows my Lord to me!

Christians with the most spiritual depth are generally those who have been taken through the most intense and deeply anguishing fires of the soul. If you have been praying to know more of Christ, do not be surprised if He leads you through the desert or through a furnace of pain.

Dear Lord, do not punish me by removing my cross from me. Instead, comfort me by leading me into submission to Your will and by causing me to love the cross. Give me only what will serve You best, and may it be used to reveal the greatest of all Your mercies: bringing glory to Your name through me, according to Your will. A CAPTIVE'S PRAYER

A thousand promises

Against all hope, Abraham in hope believed.
(ROMANS 4:18)

Abraham's faith seemed to be in complete agreement with the power and constant faithfulness of Jehovah. By looking at the outer circumstances in which he was placed, he had no reason to expect the fulfillment of God's promise. Yet he believed the Word of the Lord and looked forward to the time when his descendants would be "as numerous as the stars in the sky" (Gen. 26:4).

Dear soul, you have not been given only one promise, like Abraham, *but a thousand promises.* And you have been given the example of many faithful believers as a pattern for your life. Therefore it is simply to your advantage to rely with confidence upon the Word of God. And although He may delay in sending His help, and the evil you are experiencing may seem to become worse and worse, do not be weak. Instead, be strong and rejoice, for God usually steps forward to save us when we least expect it, fulfilling His most glorious promises in a miraculous way.

He generally waits to send His help until the time of our greatest need, so that His hand will be plainly seen in our deliverance. He chooses this method so we will not trust anything that we may see or feel, as we are so prone to do, but will place our trust solely on His Word—which we may always depend upon, no matter our circumstance. C. H. Von Bogatzky

Remember, the very time for faith to work is when our sight begins to fail. And the greater the difficulties, the easier it is for faith to work, for as long as we can see certain natural solutions to our problems, we will not have faith. Faith never works as easily as when our natural prospects fail.

George Mueller

when we are tested

We were under great pressure.
(2 CORINTHIANS 1:8)

... so that Christ's power may rest on me.
(2 CORINTHIANS 12:9)

God allowed the crisis in Jacob's life at Peniel to totally surround him until he ultimately came to the point of making an earnest and humble appeal to God Himself. That night, he wrestled with God and literally came to the place where he could take hold of Him as never before. And through his narrow brush with danger, Jacob's faith and knowledge of God was expanded, and his power to live a new and victorious life was born.

The Lord had to force David, through the discipline of many long and painful years, to learn of the almighty power and faithfulness of his God. Through those difficult years, he also grew in his knowledge of faith and godliness, which were indispensable principles for his glorious career as the king of Israel.

Nothing but the most dangerous circumstances in which Paul was constantly placed could ever have taught him, and thus the church through him, the full meaning of the great promise of God he learned to claim: "My grace is sufficient for you" (2 Cor. 12:9). And nothing but the great trials and dangers we have experienced would ever have led some of us to know Him as we do, to trust Him as we have, and to draw from Him the great measure of His grace so indispensable during our times of greatest need.

Difficulties and obstacles are God's challenges to our faith. When we are confronted with hindrances that block our path of service, we are to recognize them as vessels for faith and then to fill them with the fullness and complete sufficiency of Jesus. As we move forward in faith, simply and fully trusting Him, we may be tested. Sometimes we may have to wait and realize that "perseverance must finish its work" (James 1:4). But ultimately we will surely find "the stone rolled away" (Luke 24:2) and the Lord Himself waiting to bestow a double blessing on us for our time of testing. A. B. SIMPSON

god's time for mercy will come

And will not God bring about justice for his chosen ones, who cry out to him day and night? Will he keep putting them off? I tell you, he will see that they get justice, and quickly.

(LUKE 18:6–8)

God's timing is not ours to command. If we do not start the fire with the first strike of our match, we must try again. God does hear our prayer, but He may not answer it at the precise time we have appointed in our own minds. Instead, He will reveal Himself to our seeking hearts, though not necessarily when and where we may expect. Therefore we have a need for perseverance and steadfast determination in our life of prayer.

In the old days of flint, steel, and brimstone matches, people had to strike the match again and again, perhaps even dozens of times, before they could get a spark to light their fire, and they were very thankful if they finally succeeded. Should we not exercise the same kind of perseverance and hope regarding heavenly things? When it comes to faith, we have more certainty of success than we could ever have had with flint and steel, for we have God's promises as a foundation.

May we, therefore, never despair. God's time for mercy will come—in fact, it has already come, if our time for believing has arrived. Ask in faith without wavering, but never cease to petition the King simply because He has delayed His reply. Strike the match again and make the sparks fly. Yet be sure to have your tinder ready, for you will get a fire before long.

CHARLES H. SPURGEON

I do not believe there is such a thing in the history of God's eternal kingdom as a right prayer, offered in the right spirit, that remains forever unanswered. THEODORE L. CUYLER

wait in quiet patience

Blessed is the one who waits.
(DANIEL 12:12)

Waiting may seem like an easy thing to do, but it is a discipline that a Christian soldier does not learn without years of training. Marching and drills are much easier for God's warriors than standing still.

There are times of indecision and confusion, when even the most willing person, who eagerly desires to serve the Lord, does not know what direction to take. So what should you do when you find yourself in this situation? Should you allow yourself to be overcome with despair? Should you turn back in cowardice or in fear or rush ahead in ignorance?

No, you should simply wait—but *wait in prayer.* Call upon God and plead your case before Him, telling Him of your difficulty and reminding Him of His promise to help.

Wait in faith. Express your unwavering confidence in Him. And believe that even if He keeps you waiting until midnight, He will come at the right time to fulfill His vision for you.

Wait in quiet patience. Never complain about what you believe to be the cause of your problems, as the children of Israel did against Moses. Accept your situation exactly as it is and then simply place it with your whole heart into the hand of your covenant God. And while removing any self-will, say to Him, "Lord, 'Not my will, but yours be done' [Luke 22:42]. I do not know what to do, and I am in great need. But I will wait until You divide the flood before me or drive back my enemies. I will wait even if You keep me here many days, for my heart is fixed on You alone, dear Lord. And my spirit will wait for You with full confidence that You will still be my joy and my salvation, 'for you have been my refuge, [and] a strong tower against the foe' (Ps. 61:3)." FROM MORNING BY MORNING

Wait, patiently wait,
God never is late;
Your budding plans are in Your Father's holding,
And only wait His grand divine unfolding.
Then wait, wait,
Patiently wait.
Trust, hopefully trust,
That God will adjust
Your tangled life; and from its dark concealings,
Will bring His will, in all its bright revealings.
Then trust, trust,
Hopefully trust.
Rest, peacefully rest
On your Savior's breast;
Breathe in His ear your sacred high ambition,

And He will bring it forth in blest fruition.
   Then rest, rest,
   Peacefully rest!

MERCY A. GLADWIN

The upper and Lower springs

Caleb asked her, "What can I do for you?" She replied,
"Do me a special favor. Since you have given me
land in the Negev, give me also springs of water."
So Caleb gave her the upper and lower springs.
(JOSHUA 15:18–19)

There are both "upper and lower springs" in life, and they are *springs,* not stagnant pools. They are the joys and blessings that flow from heaven above, through the hottest summer and through the most barren desert of sorrow and trials. The land belonging to Acsah was in the Negev under the scorching sun and was often parched from the burning heat. But from the hills came the inexhaustible springs that cooled, refreshed, and fertilized all the land.

   These springs flow through the low places, the difficult places, the desert places, the lonely places, and even the ordinary places of life. And no matter what our situation may be, these springs can always be found. Abraham found them amid the hills of Canaan. Moses found them among the rocks of Midian. David found them among the ashes of Ziklag, when his property was gone and his family had been taken captive. And although his "men were talking of stoning him ... David found strength in the LORD his God" (1 Sam. 30:6).

Isaiah found them in the terrible days when King Sennacherib of Assyria invaded Judah, when the mountains themselves seemed to be thrown into the midst of the sea. Yet his faith could still sing: "There is a river whose streams make glad the city of God, the holy place where the Most High dwells. God is within her, she will not fall" (Ps. 46:4–5).

The Christian martyrs found them amid the flames, the church reformers amid their enemies and struggles, and we can find them each day of the year if we have the Comforter in our hearts and have learned to say with David, *"All my springs of joy are in you"* (Ps. 87:7 NASB).

How plentiful and how precious these springs are, and how much more there is to be possessed of God's own fullness!

A. B. SIMPSON

I said, "The desert is so wide!"
I said, "The desert is so bare!
What springs to quench my thirst are there?
Where will I from the tempest hide?"
I said, "The desert is so lone!
No gentle voice, nor loving face
To brighten any smallest space."
I paused before my cry was done!
I heard the flow of hidden springs;
Before me palms rose green and fair;
The birds were singing; all the air
Was filled and stirred with angels' wings!
And one asked softly, "Why, indeed,
Take overanxious thought for what
Tomorrow brings you? See you not
The Father knows just what you need?"

suffering and the perfecting of character

"Is your husband all right? Is your child all right?"
"Everything is all right," she said.
(2 KINGS 4:26)

Be strong, my soul!
Your loved ones go
Within the veil. God's yours, e'en so;
    Be strong.
Be strong, my soul!
Death looms in view.
Lo, hear your God! He'll bear you through;
    Be strong.

For sixty-two years and five months I had my beloved wife, and now, in my ninety-second year, I am left alone. But I turn to the ever present Jesus as I walk around my room, and say, "Lord Jesus, I am alone. Yet I am not alone, for You are with me and are my Friend. Now, Lord, please comfort me, strengthen me, and give to Your poor servant everything that You see I need."

    We should never be satisfied until we have come to the place where we know the Lord Jesus in this way—until we have discovered He is our eternal Friend—continually, under all circumstances, and constantly ready to prove Himself as our Friend. George Mueller

Afflictions cannot injure when we blend them with submission. Ice on trees will bend many a branch to the point of breaking. Similarly, I see a great many people bowed down and crushed by their afflictions. Yet every now and then I meet someone who sings in affliction, and then I thank God for my own circumstance as well as his. There is never a song more beautiful than that which is sung in the night. You may remember the story of a woman who, when her only child died, looked toward heaven as with the face of an angel and said, "I give you joy, my sweet child." That solitary, simple sentence has stayed with me for many years, often energizing and comforting me. Henry Ward Beecher

E'en for the dead I will not bind my soul to grief;
Death cannot long divide.
For is it not as though the rose that climbed my garden wall
Has blossomed on the other side?
Death does hide,
But not divide;
You are but on Christ's other side!
You are with Christ, and Christ with me;
In Christ united still are we.

the secret place

He went up on a mountainside by himself to pray.
(MATTHEW 14:23)

One of the blessings of the old-time Sabbath day was the calmness, restfulness, and holy peace that came from having a time of quiet solitude away from the world. There is a special strength that is born in solitude. Crows travel in flocks, and wolves in packs, but the lion and the eagle are usually found alone.

Strength is found not in busyness and noise but in quietness. For a lake to reflect the heavens on its surface, it must be calm. Our Lord loved the people who flocked to him, but there are numerous accounts in the Scriptures of His going away from them for a brief period of time. On occasion He would withdraw from the crowd and quite often would spend His evenings alone in the hills. Most of His ministry was performed in the towns and cities by the seashore, but He loved the hills more and at nightfall would frequently seclude Himself in their peaceful heights.

The one thing we need today more than anything else is to spend time alone with our Lord, sitting at His feet in the sacred privacy of His blessed presence. Oh, how we need to reclaim the lost art of meditation! Oh, how we need "the secret place" (Ps. 91:1 KJV) as part of our lifestyle! Oh, how we need the power that comes from waiting upon God!

Every life that desires to be strong must have its "Most Holy Place" (Ex. 26:33) into which only God enters.

It is good to live in the valley sweet,
  Where the work of the world is done,
Where the reapers sing in the fields of wheat,
  And work till the setting of the sun.
But beyond the meadows, the hills I see
  Where the noises of traffic cease,
And I follow a Voice who calls out to me
  From the hilltop regions of peace.
Yes, to live is sweet in the valley fair,
  And work till the setting of the sun;
But my spirit yearns for the hilltop's air
  When the day and its work are done.
For a Presence breathes o'er the silent hills,
  And its sweetness is living yet;
The same deep calm all the hillside fills,
  As breathed over Olivet.

Delayed Answers Are Not Refusals

But the dove could find no place to set its feet ...
so it returned to Noah in the ark.... He waited
seven more days and again sent out the dove from
the ark. When the dove returned to him in the
evening, there in its beak was a freshly plucked
olive leaf!
(GENESIS 8:9–11)

God knows exactly when to withhold or to grant us any visible sign of encouragement. How wonderful it is when we will trust Him in either case! Yet it is better when all visible evidence that He is remembering us is withheld. He wants us to realize that His Word—His promise of remembering us— is more real and dependable than any evidence our senses may reveal. It is good when He sends the visible evidence, but we appreciate it even more after we have trusted Him without it. And those who are the most inclined to trust God without any evidence except His Word always receive the greatest amount of visible evidence of His love. CHARLES GALLAUDET TRUMBULL

Believing Him; if storm clouds gather darkly 'round,
And even if the heavens seem hushed, without a sound?
He hears each prayer and even notes the sparrow's fall.

And praising Him; when sorrow, grief, and pain are near,
And even when we lose the thing that seems most dear?
Our loss is gain. Praise Him; in Him we have our All.
Our hand in His; e'en though the path seems long
    and drear
We scarcely see a step ahead, and almost fear?
He guides us right—this way and that, to keep us near.
And satisfied; when every path is blocked and bare,
And worldly things are gone and dead which were so fair?
Believe and rest and trust in Him, He comes to stay.

Delayed answers to prayers are not refusals. Many prayers are received and recorded, yet underneath are the words, "My time has not yet come." God has a fixed time and an ordained purpose, and He who controls the limits of our lives also determines the time of our deliverance.

striking the strings of your Heart

I am jealous for you with a godly jealousy.
(2 CORINTHIANS 11:2)

Oh, how the old harpist loves his harp! He cuddles and caresses it, as if it were a child resting on his lap. His life is consumed with it. But watch how he tunes it. He grasps it firmly, striking a chord with a sharp, quick blow. While it quivers as if in pain, he leans forward, intently listening to catch the first note rising from it. Just as he feared, the note is distorted and shrill. He strains the string, turning the torturing thumbscrew, and though it seems ready to snap with the tension, he strikes it again. Then he leans forward again, carefully listening, until at last a smile appears on his face as the first melodic sound arises.

Perhaps this is how God is dealing with you. Loving you more than any harpist loves his harp, He finds you nothing but harsh, discordant sounds. He plucks your heartstrings with torturing anguish. Tenderly leaning over you, he strikes the strings and listens. Hearing only a harsh murmur, He strikes you again. His heart bleeds for you while He anxiously waits to hear the strain "Not my will, but yours be done" (Luke 22:42)—a melody as sweet to His ears as angels' songs. And He will never cease from striking the strings of your heart until your humbled and disciplined soul blends with all the pure and eternal harmonies of His own being.

Oh, the sweetness that dwells in a harp of many strings,
While each, all vocal with love in a tuneful harmony rings!
But, oh, the wail and the discord, when one and another
   is rent,
Tensionless, broken and lost, from the cherished instrument.
For rapture of love is linked with the pain or fear of loss,
And the hand that takes the crown, must ache with many
   a cross;
Yet he who has never a conflict, wins never a victor's palm,
And only the toilers know the sweetness of rest and calm.
Only between the storms can the Alpine traveler know
Transcendent glory of clearness, marvels of gleam and glow;
Had he the brightness unbroken of cloudless summer days,
This had been dimmed by the dust and the veil of a
   brooding haze.
Who would dare the choice, neither or both to know,
The finest quiver of joy or the agony thrill of woe!
Never the exquisite pain, then never the exquisite bliss,
For the heart that is dull to that can never be strung to this.

a constant calm

God is in the midst of her, she will not be moved;
God will help her when morning dawns.
(PSALM 46:5 NASB)

"Will not be moved"—what an inspiring declaration! Is it possible for us who are so easily moved by earthly things to come to a point where nothing can upset us or disturb our peace? The answer is yes, and the apostle Paul knew it. When he was on his way to Jerusalem, the Holy Spirit warned him that "prison and hardships" (Acts 20:23) awaited him. Yet he could triumphantly say, "But none of these things move me" (Acts 20:24 KJV).

Everything in Paul's life and experience that could be disturbed had already been shaken, and he no longer considered his life or any of his possessions as having any earthly value. And if we will only let God have His way with us, we can come to the same point. Then, like Paul, neither the stress and strain of little things nor the great and heavy trials of life will have enough power to move us from "the peace of God, which transcends all understanding" (Phil. 4:7). God declares this peace to be the inheritance of those who have learned to rest only on Him.

"Him who overcomes I will make a pillar in the temple of my God. Never again will he leave it" (Rev. 3:12).

Becoming as immovable as a pillar in the house of God is such a worthy objective that we would gladly endure all the necessary trials that take us there! HANNAH WHITALL SMITH

When God is the center of a kingdom or a city, He makes it strong "like Mount Zion, which cannot be shaken" (Ps. 125:1). And when God is the center of a soul, although disasters may crowd in on all sides and roar like the waves of the sea, there is a constant calm within. The world can neither give nor take away this kind of peace. What is it that causes people to shake like leaves today at the first hint of danger? It is simply the lack of God living in their soul, and having the world in their hearts instead. R. LEIGHTON

"Those who trust in the LORD are like Mount Zion, which cannot be shaken but endures forever" (Ps. 125:1).

There is an old Scottish version of this psalm that strengthens our blood like iron:

Who clings to God in constant trust
As Zion's mount he stands full just,
And who moves not, nor yet does reel,
But stands forever strong as steel!

say no to "suppose"

Trust in the LORD and do good; dwell in the land and enjoy safe pasture.
(PSALM 37:3)

I once met a poor woman who earned a meager living through hard domestic labor but was a joyful, triumphant Christian. Another Christian lady, who was quite sullen, said to her one day, "Nancy, I understand your happiness today, but I would think your future prospects would sober you. Suppose, for instance, you experience a time of illness and are unable to work. Or suppose your present employers move away, and you cannot find work elsewhere. Or suppose—"

"Stop!" cried Nancy. "I never 'suppose.' 'The LORD is my shepherd, I shall not be in want' [Ps. 23:1]. And besides," she added to her gloomy friend, "it's all that 'supposing' that's making you so miserable. You'd better give that up and simply trust the Lord."

The following Scripture is one that will remove all the "supposing" from a believer's life if received and acted on in childlike faith: "Be content with what you have, because God has said, 'Never will I leave you; never will I forsake you.' So we say with confidence, 'The Lord is my helper; I will not be afraid. What can man do to me?'" (Heb. 13:5–6).

HANNAH WHITALL SMITH

There's a stream of trouble across my path;
  It is dark and deep and wide.
Bitter the hour the future hath
  When I cross its swelling tide.
But I smile and sing and say:
  "I will hope and trust alway;
I'll bear the sorrow that comes tomorrow,
  But I'll borrow none today."
Tomorrow's bridge is a dangerous thing;
  I dare not cross it now.
I can see its timbers sway and swing,
  And its arches reel and bow.
O heart, you must hope alway;
  You must sing and trust and say:
"I'll bear the sorrow that comes tomorrow,
  But I'll borrow none today."

The eagle that soars at great altitudes does not worry about how it will cross a river.

Taking possession of God's promises

*I will give you every place where you set your foot,
as I promised.*
(JOSHUA 1:3)

Besides the literal ground still unoccupied for Christ, there is
before us the unclaimed and unwalked territory of *God's
promises*. What did God say to Joshua? "I will give you *every
place* where you set your foot, *as I promised*." Then He set
the boundaries of the Land of Promise—all theirs on one
condition: *they must march across its length and breadth*,
measuring it off with their own feet.

Yet they never marched across more than one third of
the land, and as a consequence, they never *possessed* more than
that one third. They possessed only what they measured off
and no more.

In 2 Peter 1:4 we read, "He has given us his very great and
precious promises." The land of God's promises is open before
us, and it is His will for us to possess it. We must measure off
the territory with the feet of obedient faith and faithful
obedience, thereby claiming and appropriating it as our own.

How many of us have ever taken possession of the promises
of God in the name of Christ? The land of His promises is a
magnificent territory for faith to claim by marching across its
length and breadth, but faith has yet to do it.

Let us enter into and claim our total inheritance. Let us lift our eyes to the north, south, east, and west and hear God say, "All the land that you see I will give to you" (Gen. 13:15).
ARTHUR TAPPAN PIERSON

Wherever the tribe of Judah set their feet would be theirs, and wherever the tribe of Benjamin set their feet would be theirs, and so on. Each tribe would receive their inheritance by setting foot upon it. Don't you imagine that as each tribe set foot upon a given territory, they instantly and instinctively felt, "This is ours"?

An elderly black man who had a wonderful testimony of grace was once asked, "Daniel, how is it that you exhibit such peace and joy in your faith?" "Oh, sir!" he replied. "I just fall flat on God's 'very great and precious promises,' and I have all that is in them. Glory! Glory!" One who falls flat on God's promises knows that all the riches abiding in them are his.
FROM FAITH PAPERS

The Marquis of Salisbury, an English statesman and diplomat, upon being criticized for his colonial policies, replied, "Gentlemen, get larger maps."

quietness in the midst
of the raging storm

He giveth quietness.

(JOB 34:29 KJV)

He gives quietness in the midst of the raging storm. As we sail the lake with Him, reaching deep water and far from land, suddenly, under the midnight sky, a mighty storm sweeps down. Earth and hell seem mobilized against us, and each wave threatens to overwhelm our boat. Then He rises from His sleep and rebukes the wind and the waves. He waves His hand, signaling the end of the raging tempest and the beginning of the restful calm. His voice is heard above the screaming of the wind through the ropes and rigging, and over the thrashing of the waves. "Quiet! Be still!" (Mark 4:39). Can you not hear it? And instantly there is a great calm.

"He giveth quietness"—*quietness even in the midst of losing our inner strength and comforts.* Sometimes He removes these because we make too much of them. We are tempted to look at our joys, pleasures, passions, or our dreams, with too much self-satisfaction. Then through His gracious love He withdraws them, leading us to distinguish between them and Himself. He draws near and whispers the assurance of His presence, bringing an infinite calm to keep our hearts and minds. "He giveth quietness."

"He giveth quietness." O Elder Brother,
  Whose homeless feet have pressed our path of pain,
Whose hands have borne the burden of our sorrow,
  That in our losses we might find our gain.
Of all Your gifts and infinite consolings,
  I ask but this: in every troubled hour
To hear Your voice through all the tumults stealing,
  And rest serene beneath its tranquil power.
Cares cannot fret me if my soul be dwelling
  In the still air of faith's untroubled day;
Grief cannot shake me if I walk beside You,
  My hand in Yours along the darkening way.
Content to know there comes a radiant morning
  When from all shadows I will find release;
Serene to wait the rapture of its dawning—
  Who can make trouble when You send me peace?

The shepherd who "goes on ahead"

When he has brought out all his own, he goes on ahead of them.

(JOHN 10:4)

This is intensely difficult work for Him and us—it is difficult for us to go, but equally difficult for Him to cause us pain. Yet it must be done. It would not be in our best interest to always remain in one happy and comfortable location. Therefore He moves us forward. The shepherd leaves the fold so the sheep will move on to the vitalizing mountain slopes. In the same way, laborers must be driven out into the harvest, or else the golden grain would spoil.

But take heart! It could never be better to stay once He determines otherwise; if the loving hand of our Lord moves us forward, it must be best. Forward, in His name, to green pastures, quiet waters, and mountain heights! (See Ps. 23:2.) "He goes on ahead of [us]." So whatever awaits us is encountered first by Him, and the eye of faith can always discern His majestic presence out in front. When His presence cannot be seen, it is dangerous to move ahead. Comfort your heart with the fact that the Savior has Himself experienced all the trials He asks you to endure; He would not ask you to pass through them unless He was sure that the paths were not too difficult or strenuous for you.

This is the blessed life—not anxious to see far down the road nor overly concerned about the next step, not eager to choose the path nor weighted down with the heavy responsibilities of the future, but quietly following the Shepherd, one step at a time.

Dark is the sky! and veiled the unknown morrow!
Dark is life's way, for night is not yet o'er;
The longed-for glimpse I may not meanwhile borrow;
But, this I know and trust, HE GOES BEFORE.
Dangers are near! and fears my mind are shaking;
Heart seems to dread what life may hold in store;
But I am His—He knows the way I'm taking,
More blessed even still—HE GOES BEFORE.
Doubts cast their weird, unwelcome shadows o'er me,
Doubts that life's best—life's choicest things are o'er;
What but His Word can strengthen, can restore me,
And this blest fact; that still HE GOES BEFORE.
HE GOES BEFORE! Be this my consolation!
He goes before! On this my heart would dwell!
He goes before! This guarantees salvation!
HE GOES BEFORE! And therefore all is well.

J. DANSON SMITH

The oriental shepherd always walked ahead of his sheep. He was always out in front. Any attack upon the sheep had to take him into account first. Now God is out in front. He is in our tomorrows, and it is tomorrow that fills people with fear. Yet God is already there. All the tomorrows of our life have to pass through Him before they can get to us. F. B. Meyer

God is in every tomorrow,
    Therefore I live for today,
Certain of finding at sunrise,
    Guidance and strength for my way;
Power for each moment of weakness,
    Hope for each moment of pain,
Comfort for every sorrow,
    Sunshine and joy after rain.

our god—"the living god"

Daniel, servant of the living God, has your God, whom you serve continually, been able to rescue you?
(DANIEL 6:20)

We find the expression "the living God" many times in the Scriptures, and yet it is the very thing we are so prone to forget. We know it is written "the living God," but in our daily life there is almost nothing we lose sight of as often as the fact that God is the living God. We forget that He is now exactly what He was three or four thousand years ago, that He has the same sovereign power, and that He extends the same gracious love toward those who love and serve Him. We overlook the fact that He will do for us now what He did thousands of years ago for others, simply because He is the unchanging, living God. What a great reason to confide in Him, and in our darkest moments to never lose sight of the fact that He is still, and ever will be, the living God!

Be assured, if you walk with Him, look to Him, and expect help from Him, He will never fail you. An older believer who has known the Lord for forty-four years wrote the following as an encouragement to you: "God has never failed me. Even in my greatest difficulties, heaviest trials, and deepest poverty and need, He has never failed me. Because I was enabled by God's grace to trust Him, He has always come to my aid. I delight in speaking well of His name." GEORGE MUELLER

Martin Luther, deep in thought and needing to grasp hidden strength during a time of danger and fear in his life, was seen tracing on the table with his finger the words, "He lives! He lives!" This is our hope for ourselves, His truth, and humankind. People come and go. Leaders, teachers, and philosophers speak and work for a season and then fall silent and powerless. He abides. They die but He lives. They are lights that glow yet are ultimately extinguished. But He is the true Light from which they draw their brightness, and He shines forevermore. ALEXANDER MACLAREN

"One day I came to know Dr. John Douglas Adam," wrote Charles Gallaudet Trumbull. "I learned he considered his greatest spiritual asset to be his unwavering awareness of the actual presence of Jesus. Nothing sustained him as much, he said, as the realization that Jesus was always actually present with him. This realization was totally independent of his own feelings, his worthiness, and his perceptions as to how Jesus would demonstrate His presence.

"Furthermore, he said Christ was the center of his thoughts. Whenever his mind was free from other matters, it would turn to Christ. Whenever he was alone, and no matter where he was, he would talk aloud to Christ as easily and as naturally as to any human friend. That is how very real Jesus' actual presence was to him."

A steadfast commitment to christ

Make you strong, firm and steadfast.
(1 PETER 5:10)

Before we can establish a new and deeper relationship with Christ, we must first acquire enough intellectual light to satisfy our mind that we have been given the right to stand in this new relationship. Even the shadow of a doubt here will destroy our confidence. Then, having seen the light, we must advance. We must make our choice, commit to it, and take our rightful place as confidently as a tree is planted in the ground. As a bride entrusts herself to the groom at the marriage altar, our commitment to Christ must be once and for all, without reservation or reversal.

Then there follows a time of establishing and testing, during which we must stand still until the new relationship becomes so ingrained in us that it becomes a permanent habit. It is comparable to a surgeon setting a broken arm by splinting it to keep it from moving. God too has His spiritual splints He wants to put on His children to keep them quiet and still until they pass the first stage of faith. Sometimes the trial will be difficult, but "the God of all grace, who called you to his eternal glory in Christ, after you have suffered a little while, will himself restore you and make you strong, firm and steadfast" (1 Peter 5:10). A. B. SIMPSON

There is a natural law at work in sin and in sickness, and if we just drift along following the flow of our circumstances, we will sink under the power of the Tempter. But there is another law of spiritual and physical life in Christ Jesus to which we can rise, and through which we can counterbalance and overcome the natural law that weighs us down.

Doing this, however, requires real spiritual energy, a determined purpose, a sure stance, and the habit of faith. It is the same principle as a factory that uses electricity to run its machinery. The switch must be turned on and left in that position. The power is always available, but the proper connection must be made. And as long as that connection is intact, the power will enable all the machinery to stay in operation.

There is a spiritual law of choosing, believing, abiding, and remaining steadfast in our walk with God. This law is essential to the working of the Holy Spirit in our sanctification and in our healing. FROM DAYS OF HEAVEN UPON EARTH

The shepherd who is always there

Surely I am with you always.
(MATTHEW 28:20)

Never look ahead to the changes and challenges of this life in fear. Instead, as they arise look at them with the full assurance that God, whose you are, will deliver you out of them. Hasn't He kept you safe up to now? So hold His loving hand tightly, and He will lead you safely through all things. And when you cannot stand, He will carry you in His arms.

Do not look ahead to what may happen tomorrow. The same everlasting Father who cares for you today will take care of you tomorrow and every day. Either He will shield you from suffering or He will give you His unwavering strength that you may bear it. Be at peace, then, and set aside all anxious thoughts and worries. FRANCIS DE SALES

The LORD is my shepherd. PSALM 23:1

Not was, not may be, nor will be. "The LORD is my shepherd." He is on Sunday, on Monday, and through every day of the week. He is in January, in December, and every month of the year. He is when I'm at home and in China. He is during peace or war, and in times of abundance or poverty. J. HUDSON TAYLOR

HE will silently plan for you,
His object of omniscient care;
God Himself undertakes to be
Your Pilot through each subtle snare.
He WILL silently plan for you,
So certainly, He cannot fail!
Rest on the faithfulness of God,
In Him you surely will prevail.
He will SILENTLY plan for you
Some wonderful surprise of love.
No eye has seen, no ear has heard,
But it is kept for you above.
He will silently PLAN for you,
His purposes will all unfold;
Your tangled life will shine at last,
A masterpiece of skill untold.

He will silently plan FOR YOU,
    Happy child of a Father's care,
As if no other claimed His love,
    But you alone to Him were dear.

E. MARY GRIMES

Whatever our faith says God is, He will be.

The Lord—our Eternal Help

Thus far has the Lord helped us.
(1 SAMUEL 7:12)

The words "thus far" are like a hand pointing in the direction of the past. It had been "a long time, twenty years in all" (v. 2), but even if it had been seventy years, "Thus far has the Lord helped"! Whether through poverty, wealth, sickness, or health, whether at home or abroad, or on land, sea, or air, and whether in honor, dishonor, difficulties, joy, trials, triumph, prayer, or temptation— "Thus far has the Lord helped"!

We always enjoy looking down a long road lined with beautiful trees. The trees are a delightful sight and seem to be forming a temple of plants, with strong wooden pillars and arches of leaves. In the same way you look down a beautiful road like this, why not look back on the road of the years of your life? Look at the large green limbs of God's mercy overhead and the strong pillars of His loving-kindness and faithfulness that have brought you much joy. Do you see any birds singing in the branches? If you look closely, surely you will see many, for they are singing of God's mercy received "thus far."

These words also point forward. Someone who comes to a certain point and writes the words "thus far" realizes he has not yet come to the end of the road and that he still has some distance to travel. There are still more trials, joys, temptations, battles, defeats, victories, prayers, answers, toils, and strength yet to come. These are then followed by sickness, old age, disease, and death.

Then is life over after death? No! These are still yet to come: arising in the likeness of Jesus; thrones, harps, and the singing of psalms; being "clothed in white garments" (Rev. 3:5 NASB), seeing the face of Jesus, and sharing fellowship with the saints; and experiencing the glory of God, the fullness of eternity, and infinite joy. So dear believer, "be strong and take heart" (Ps. 27:14), and with thanksgiving and confidence lift your voice in praise, for:

The Lord who "thus far" has helped you
Will help you all your journey through.

When the words "thus far" are read in heaven's light, what glorious and miraculous prospects they reveal to our grateful eyes! CHARLES H. SPURGEON

The shepherds of the Alps have a beautiful custom of ending the day by singing an evening farewell to one another. The air is so pure that the songs can be heard for very long distances. As the sun begins to set, they gather their flocks and begin to lead them down the mountain paths while they sing, " 'Thus far has the LORD helped us.' Let us praise His name!"

Finally, as is their beautiful custom, they sing to one another the courteous and friendly farewell "Goodnight! Goodnight!" The words then begin to echo from mountainside to mountainside, reverberating sweetly and softly until the music fades into the distance.

Let us also call out to one another through the darkness until the night becomes alive with the sound of many voices, encouraging God's weary travelers. And may the echoes grow into a storm of hallelujahs that will break in thundering waves around His sapphire throne. Then as the morning dawns, we will find ourselves on the shore of the "sea of glass" (Rev. 4:6), crying out with the redeemed hosts of heaven, "To him who sits on the throne and to the Lamb be praise and honor and glory and power, for ever and ever!" (Rev. 5:13).

This my song through endless ages,
    Jesus led me all the way.
AND AGAIN THEY SHOUTED: "HALLELUJAH!"
                                REVELATION 19:3

At Inspirio we love to hear from you—
your stories, your feedback,
and your product ideas.
Please send your comments to us
by way of email at
icares@zondervan.com
or to the address below:

inspirio™

Attn: Inspirio Cares
5300 Patterson Avenue SE
Grand Rapids, MI 49530

If you would like further information
about Inspirio and the products we
create please visit us at:
www.inspiriogifts.com

Thank you and God bless!